D0209653

WHY THE TEN COMMANDMENTS MATTER

WHY THE TEN COMMANDMENTS MATTER

D. JAMES KENNEDY
with David Hazard

NEW YORK BOSTON NASHVILLE

Copyright © 2005 by D. James Kennedy
All rights reserved.

Unless otherwise noted, Scriptures are taken from the NEW KING JAMES VERSION. Copyright © 1979, 1980, 1982, Thomas Nelson, Inc., Publishers.
Scriptures noted NIV are taken from the HOLY BIBLE: NEW INTERNATIONAL VERSION®. Copyright © 1973, 1978, 1984 by International Bible Society. Used by permission of Zondervan Publishing House. All rights reserved.
Scriptures noted KJV are taken from the King James Version of the Bible.
Scriptures noted NASB are taken from the New American Standard Bible®, Copyright © 1960, 1962, 1963, 1968, 1972, 1975, 1977, 1995 by The Lockman Foundation. Used by permission.

Editorial development by Hazard Communications, Inc.

Coral Ridge Ministries
P.O. Box 40
Fort Lauderdale, FL 33302
letters@coralridge.org
www.crm.tv

Warner Faith

Time Warner Book Group
1271 Avenue of the Americas, New York, NY 10020
Visit our Web site at www.twbookmark.com

Warner Faith® and the Warner Faith logo are trademarks of
Time Warner Book Group Inc.

Printed in the United States of America

Originally published as *God's Best for You*
First Warner Faith Edition: May 2005
10 9 8 7 6 5 4 3 2 1

Library of Congress Cataloging-in-Publication Data

Kennedy, D. James (Dennis James).
Why the Ten commandments matter / D. James Kennedy.— 1st ed.
p. cm.
"A meditative examination of the value of the Ten Commandments in today's America" — Provided by the publisher.
ISBN 0-446-57727-8
1. Ten commandments—Criticism, interpretation, etc. I. Title.
BS1285.52.K46 2005
241.5'2—dc22 2004026474

CONTENTS

CONCORDIA UNIVERSITY LIBRARY
PORTLAND, OR 97211

INTRODUCTION

Each year in May, many Americans join in a National Day of Prayer. This annual event, established by Congress, is the day on which our nation—or some portion of it, at any rate—turns to God in prayer.

On this particular day of the year, we focus on one of the most impassioned types of praying we can undertake. I am referring to prayer for the repentance, forgiveness, and healing of our great land. We intercede on behalf of our nation, quoting and trusting in the words of one of God's great promises to His people:

> If my people, who are called by my name, will humble themselves and pray and seek my face and turn from their wicked ways, then will I hear from heaven and will forgive their sin and will heal their land (2 Chronicles 7:14, NIV).

We are right to pray for our nation—not only on that day, but on every day of the year. If we consider the state of affairs we are in, morally speaking, it is terrible, indeed.

The sin for which we are beseeching God's forgiveness is, in fact, rampant in America.

A few years ago, William Bennett's *The Index of Leading Cultural Indicators* documented our nation's deplorable moral condition with a mountain of evidence. Bennett reported,

- America has the highest divorce rate of any industrialized nation.
- Forty out of every 100 first marriages end in divorce.
- Roughly one in every four pregnancies ends at an abortion clinic rather than in a delivery room.
- Fifty percent of children will spend their entire childhood in a split-family situation, emotionally wrestling with divided loyalties.
- One of every three births is out of wedlock, and single-parent families make up 32 percent of all families in America.
- The growth rate of sexually transmitted diseases in America outpaces that of every other developed nation.[1]

Sin is not only destroying individual lives and individual health, it is mercilessly bludgeoning the family in America. These conditions are cause for gloom and dismay. Surely, God's anger and judgment are due a nation that kills the innocent for personal convenience and destroys the home in the name of selfish personal "satisfaction."

Yes, we are right to pray for our nation. Our national days of prayer cannot come a moment too soon. For apart from God's mercy, we have no hope.

But hold on a moment. We who are Christians, we who are praying for the repentance of our land, would do well to look more closely at this promise from God on which we are counting so desperately. As believers, we are not exempt from the need for repentance. For the promise says, "If my people . . . will humble themselves . . . and turn from their wicked ways . . ."

Repentance from sin is the condition on which God will hear our prayers and heal our land. How tragic that we Christians seem to have ignored that part! How tragic that repentance is so desperately needed today in the Church as it kneels to pray for the repentance of the nation!

Researcher George Barna believes that evangelicals are not that different from the surrounding culture. A recent Barna Research survey found, for example, the percentage of born-again adults who have been married and divorced is now statistically equivalent to that among non-born-again adults.[2] In other words, those who claim to follow Christ are no less likely than any other single group in our culture to be divorced.

This compares with atheists and agnostics who, according to research, are the least likely of any single group in our culture to be divorced.

What on earth is going on? While we Christians are praying fervently for the repentance and healing of our nation, the Church is breaking God's commandments and contributing to the epidemic of immorality that is destroying the fabric of our nation, our families, and individual human lives. We Christians are among those most guilty when Barna declares: "America is suffering moral and spiritual anarchy." Instead of living according to the Bible, we've decided to live "according to our own rules."

The only real question we need to ask ourselves is: What are we going to do about it? Nancy Leigh DeMoss, author and editor of *Spirit of Revival* magazine, told a group of national leaders several years ago about the Church's special responsibility to be holy in a pagan culture. "The Bride has forgotten how to blush," she stated. "We sin without shame. We have lost our ability to mourn and grieve and weep over sin."[3]

I believe her assessment is correct. We have lost our shame and grief over our sins. Undoubtedly, this has occurred because we do not spend enough time in God's Word. More specifically, I believe, we in the Church stand guilty of ignoring God's moral laws, handed to us on Mount Sinai in the form of the Ten Commandments. And as we ignore and break these commandments, we stand guilty of destroying the foundations of our nation, our communities, and our homes.

If we are going to rebuild our ruined moral foundations as a nation . . . if we are going to stay God's hand of judgment . . . we Christians must allow God's Word and His commandments to search our hearts and lives and begin to set us on the path of righteousness again. It is not only the path of repentance and forgiveness, it is also the path on which we will find God's healing and grace for us and our nation.

To that end, I invite you to follow me in this exploration of God's eternal, absolute, moral law—His Ten Commandments. I know that as you explore each one—and allow each one of them to search your heart—you will find conviction and the need to turn from "wicked ways," and you will find the life of blessing and right living—God's absolute best for you.

—D. JAMES KENNEDY, PH.D.
MAY 2004

WHY THE TEN COMMANDMENTS MATTER

THE TEN COMMANDMENTS

I am the LORD your God, who brought you out of the land of Egypt, out of the house of bondage. You shall have no other gods before Me.

You shall not make for yourself a carved image—or any likeness of anything that is in heaven above, or that is in the earth beneath, or that is in the water under the earth; you shall not bow down to them nor serve them. For I, the LORD your God, am a jealous God, visiting the iniquity of the fathers upon the children to the third and fourth generations of those who hate Me, but showing mercy to thousands, to those who love Me and keep My commandments.

You shall not take the name of the LORD your God in vain, for the LORD will not hold him guiltless who takes His name in vain.

Remember the Sabbath day, to keep it holy. Six days you shall labor and do all your work, but the seventh day is the Sabbath of the LORD your God. In it you shall do no work: you, nor your son, nor your daughter, nor your male servant, nor your female servant, nor your cattle, nor your stranger who is within your gates. For in six days the LORD made the heavens and the earth, the sea, and all that is in them, and rested the seventh day. Therefore the LORD blessed the Sabbath day and hallowed it.

Honor your father and your mother, that your days may be long upon the land which the LORD your God is giving you.

You shall not murder.

You shall not commit adultery.

You shall not steal.

You shall not bear false witness against your neighbor.

You shall not covet your neighbor's house; you shall not covet your neighbor's wife, nor his male servant, nor his female servant, nor his ox, nor his donkey, nor anything that is your neighbor's.

—EXODUS 20:2-17

CHAPTER ONE

Do We Need the Law of God?

Mount Sinai was completely in smoke, because the Lord *descended upon it in fire. Its smoke ascended like the smoke of a furnace, and the whole mountain quaked greatly. And when the blast of the trumpet sounded long and became louder and louder, Moses spoke, and God answered him by voice. Then the* Lord *came down upon Mount Sinai, on the top of the mountain. And the* Lord *called Moses to the top of the mountain, and Moses went up.*

—Exodus 19:18-20

IMAGINE THAT YOU are among the vast throng of Israelites who have just been delivered from Egypt, following Moses in the great Exodus. You have seen the incredible power of God with your own eyes. You watched in awe as He rolled back the waters of the Red Sea to allow you and your countrymen to cross on dry land. Then, safely on the other side of the sea, you saw the waters come back together, covering the terrified Egyptian solders who had been pursuing you.

You have tasted the manna that God sent from heaven to feed you, and quenched your thirst with water that flowed from a rock at His command. Yes, you have seen God's power to save and heal, and you have also seen His power to destroy and kill.

And now, you stand before the mountain of God—Mount Sinai! It is shrouded in cloud and smoke, as if from a furnace. There is lightning and thunder. The mountain shakes and trembles.

And you, too, are trembling. Your heart is melting within you as you fall upon your face with all the others and cry out to Moses, "You speak with us, and we will hear; but let not God speak with us, lest we die" (Exodus 20:19).

What an incredible day it was when the Almighty came to sit, as it were, upon a gigantic throne of granite to dispense His laws to His covenant people! They were the operating instructions from the Creator. On this occasion, God did not use the voice of a prophet, but spoke with His own voice. He did not use the pen of a scribe, but wrote with His own finger upon the tablets of stone.

They were the Ten Commandments of God, His moral laws for all mankind.

And you—lying in the dust before the smoking, flaming mountain of God—would never, ever consider breaking one of them. After all, you knew what would happen to you if you did. The Israelites who followed Moses out of Egypt some 3,500 years ago feared and respected God and His laws because they saw the consequences that came from disobedience.

But since the day God wrote His laws on those tablets of stone, innumerable individuals and nations have hurled themselves against them. The remnants of their destruction may be found in the hospitals, the asylums, the prisons, the battlefields, the skid rows of this world. What was true thousands of years ago remains true today. You cannot break the law of God; you can only break yourself upon it.

Consider a small sampling of what happens when people think they are free to disregard the Ten Commandments:

Leslie met her husband, Ron, in a church youth group when both were teenagers. They fell in love and were married just three years later, shortly before Ron's twenty-first birthday. When some of their friends questioned them about the wisdom of getting married so young, Ron said that no matter how long he lived, he knew he could never love another woman as much as he loved Leslie.

That was then; this is now.

Just a few weeks ago, Leslie discovered letters tucked away in one of her husband's drawers. Her heart broke because the secret letters caused her to believe Ron had been unfaithful to her. Not once, but at least three times . . . and possibly more.

When she confronted Ron, he admitted his guilt. But that was all. He was completely unrepentant. Unwilling to break off the relationship with his current girlfriend, Ron chose to walk away from his marriage and his two young children. The kids are really too young to know what has happened, except that they miss their daddy. However, Leslie is devastated and lies awake at night, wondering how a fine young man who seemed to love God and his family with all of his heart could have slipped into this kind of lifestyle and become so callous and unfeeling toward people he once loved.

David grew up in a safe neighborhood where kids could play freely and parents didn't have to spend a lot of time worrying that they might be getting into trouble. It wasn't a rich neighborhood by any means, but it was secure, and he always felt safe. Now, thirty years later, he worries when his twelve-year-old daughter rides her bike alone in their affluent neighborhood. If she isn't home exactly when she promised, he prepares to look for her.

Is he overreacting? Not at all. He knows the statistics. He understands that thousands of children just like his daughter are kidnapped, molested, or victimized by lesser forms of violence every year. And he also knows that no neighborhood in America is truly safe.

Just last month, a student was expelled from the local high school for bringing a gun to class. David shakes his head as he remembers the America of his youth. He wonders what happened to that nation. How did we get to this point?

Dana has always thought of herself as an honest and upright person, but she has trouble telling the truth when she thinks it might hurt someone's feelings. So, when her friend Joyce called recently and asked her if she wanted to go out for dinner, she said she had a headache and was going to stay home and go to bed early. She didn't want to admit that she already had plans with someone she'd just met—a coworker from the school where she was a teacher. She justified her dishonesty by reminding herself that Joyce was easily hurt and might not understand.

She didn't count on Joyce coming over with a big pot of soup for her "sick" friend and discovering that Dana wasn't home. Talk about being hurt! And now Joyce says she feels that she can't trust Dana and no longer wants to be her friend. Dana has tried on several occasions to get things patched up, but Joyce says, "I just don't understand why you lied to me."

All Dana can say in reply is, "I don't know either, and I wish I had never done it." Sadly, she can't go back and change what has already happened.

* * *

The situations I've just mentioned are typical of those faced by thousands of people in modern American society. All around us, families are breaking up, once-safe neighborhoods are falling victim to violence and crime, and moral absolutes are being discarded whenever they get in the way. Furthermore, every one of the situations I've just described results from direct disobedience to one of God's laws.

For example, one of the Ten Commandments says, "You shall not commit adultery." Ron has broken that law, with the result that he has also broken his wife's heart and split his family apart. He has touched off a cycle of hurt and shame that will last for generations, and unless he repents and changes his ways, he will be broken eventually.

The difficulties in David's neighborhood—and in neighborhoods throughout the United States—have also occurred because the Ten Commandments are not being heeded and obeyed. God says, "You shall not murder," and "You shall not steal," but modern society—having attempted to turn its back on God's laws—has created a world where few seem to know the difference between right and wrong, and where stealing and killing are commonplace. Am I overstating the case? Hardly. For example, consider that murder isn't even front-page news anymore. In big city newspapers, the latest murders are usually relegated to tiny reports far back in Section B.

As far as Dana is concerned, she would have preserved a friendship, and she would have felt better about herself, if she had obeyed God's command not to bear false witness, which is another term for lying.

A SOCIETY TURNS AWAY FROM GOD

Sometimes it seems as if our entire society is attempting to turn away from God's laws, with very dramatic and unpleasant results. People act as if the Ten Commandments are passé—a relic from a long-gone era. But the truth is that they are the lynchpin that holds our society together.

Recently, the U.S. Supreme Court let stand a ruling forcing a small town in Indiana to remove a monument featuring the Ten Commandments in front of its city hall. What a tragic mistake! Were it up to me, I would make sure the commandments were posted in every courthouse in America—and not only in America, but all over the world! I would also make sure they were posted in a prominent location in every public school. That is why I am so pleased with the courage and conviction of Alabama Chief Justice Roy S. Moore, who placed a granite monument bearing the Ten Commandments in the rotunda of the state supreme court building. Both his courage and conviction were put to the test in 2003 when a federal judge ordered him to remove the monument. Moore refused to do so, citing the obligation imposed on him by his oath of office, and he paid the price. He was removed from office by a state judicial body, an action he has appealed to the U.S. Supreme Court.

Not long ago, a snippet of a song from the late 1960s caught my ear. If you're old enough, I'm sure you remember the hit song

"Aquarius" by a vocal group called the Fifth Dimension. The song proclaims again and again that "this is the dawning of the age of Aquarius." And it talks about all of the "love and understanding" that are going to be so much a part of everything as the world moves into a wonderful new era.

In 1969 that song sounded like an anthem of optimism. Today it sounds more like a sad, pathetic joke. What has this "age of love and understanding" brought us?

- Neighborhoods where people are afraid to venture outside because of the threat of gang violence.
- Drive-by shootings involving kids as young as twelve and thirteen years of age.
- The tragedy of Columbine High School, and a number of other shootings in schools throughout the United States.
- The tragic decimation of the family.

I am certain you can think of many more ways in which our society has regressed over the past few decades and even in the last few years. As a society, we have blatantly turned away from the Ten Commandments, and as a result, our world has become unstable, frightening, and dangerous.

GOD'S LAWS CAN NEVER BE BROKEN

Now, one reason why the age of "love and understanding" never materialized is that those who proclaimed its arrival didn't know God or understand His laws. They envisioned a world in which we would throw off the restraint of "old-fashioned" morality, forget about God, and live in complete peace, freedom, and harmony. They didn't understand that God gave us His laws for a reason. His desire has never been to hold us back or keep us from having a good time. God gave us His laws because He knew that only in following them can we achieve our full potential—which is not the potential of "enlightened, fulfilled men"—rather, it is our potential to become the obedient sons and daughters of the living God.

Dr. Paul Johnson, an eminent historian, has written a book titled *Modern Times* that chronicles the events of the twentieth century. He points out that one of the most important events of this century was the publication, in 1905, of Albert Einstein's theory of relativity.

Johnson notes that ever since that theory came to be accepted as fact in the world of physics, others have been trying to make it work in every conceivable discipline, including ethics and religion. It has been one gigantic experiment, testing whether man can live without absolutes.[1]

The answer, apparently, is that, yes, man can live without absolutes, but not very well.

Please do not misunderstand me and think that I am blaming society's slide into anarchy and relativism on Albert Einstein. The great scientist expressed his fear over where this movement would lead us when he said, "Relativity applies to physics, not ethics."

Yet for most of the twentieth century, people were willing to listen to the voice of a person like Karl Marx, who insisted that man is controlled not by the absolutes of God, but by economic factors. They nodded in agreement to Friedrich Nietzsche's proclamation that "God is dead," and therefore, the only thing that controls man is the quest for power. They marveled at the wisdom of men like Sigmund Freud, who maintained that man is controlled by sexual desire and not by the laws of God; and Charles Darwin, who vowed that the only law that really mattered was "the survival of the fittest."

What is left of the legacy these men handed down to us?

The Communist empire that was built on the teachings of Karl Marx lies in shambles—a bitter, failed experiment, leaving behind a sordid history of torture, murder, genocide, corruption, and betrayal of the innocent.

Friedrich Nietzsche? The man whose theories gave rise to the secular religion known as humanism—which would elevate man into the position of God—lived out the last years of his life in a mental institution.

Sigmund Freud is no longer revered in psychological circles. In fact, his theories are considered passé by most modern psychologists. Sadly, it is too late to undo all the damage his theories did by unleashing a sexual revolution that perverted one of God's great gifts to mankind.

And what of Darwin? His views have largely been discarded by scientists working in the field of genetics. Why? They just don't seem to fit the facts. Yet thousands of people go on blindly believing the theory of evolution rather than accepting the truth that there is a God who created the universe, just as the Bible says.

ABSOLUTE AND IMMOVABLE

The truth is that God's laws are not relative. They are absolute and they are immovable. That this is so is a fact borne out by several thousand years of world history.

At this point, you may say, "But Dr. Kennedy, didn't the sacrificial death of Jesus Christ fulfill our obligation to obey the Ten Commandments?"

We will allow our Lord Himself to answer that question from a statement recorded in the gospel of Matthew:

> Do not think that I came to destroy the Law or the Prophets. I did not come to destroy but to fulfill. For assuredly, I say to you, till heaven and earth pass away, one jot or one tittle will by no means pass from the law till all is fulfilled. Whoever therefore breaks one of the least of these commandments, and teaches men so, shall be called least in the kingdom of heaven; but whoever does and teaches them, he shall be called great in the kingdom of heaven (Matthew 5:17-19).

If we want to fully understand what Jesus was teaching in this passage, we need to understand that when God spoke to Moses on Mount Sinai, He gave three kinds of laws.

Civil Laws

The first were the civil laws—the laws of government for Israel. You see, there was no legislature or parliament in Israel to pass new laws or tack amendments onto existing ones. Israel was a theocracy, and God was the only Legislator.

When you read the Old Testament, civil laws are easy to recognize because they always mention a punishment that is incurred when they are broken, such as a fine, a beating, or an execution. No one could plead ignorance. If you broke a civil law and got caught, you knew exactly what your punishment would be, and you could count on the fact that it was going to be swift.

I think it's worth noting that there were no prisons in ancient Israel. Instead, they had cities of refuge to preclude vigilantism. The Babylonians had prisons. So did the Assyrians and the Romans. But not the Jews. They did not need prisons, because crime was dealt with quickly and, when necessary, severely.

What happened to the civil laws of the Old Testament? When Rome destroyed the theocracy of Israel in A.D 70, the civil laws were simultaneously abolished.

Ceremonial Laws

The second type of laws found in the first five books of the Old Testament were the ceremonial laws. They dealt with the sin offerings, the trespass offerings, and all of the various offerings and sacrifices of the Jewish religious system. All of these sacrifices served as a foreshadowing of Christ, the Messiah, who was yet to come.

Through faith in the atoning death of the coming Messiah, as set forth in the sacrificial offering, a sacrifice that included the blood of bulls and goats, a Hebrew of Old Testament times could have his sins temporarily covered. They could not be forgiven, but the "payment due" date could be put off for a certain period of time.

When Christ gave His life "as a ransom for many" (Matthew

20:28), that changed. There was no longer any need for ceremonial sacrifices because Jesus had paid the price for our sins once and for all (Hebrews 10:11-14). The Bible tells us that when John the Baptist saw Jesus coming toward him, he said, "Behold! The Lamb of God who takes away the sins of the world!" (John 1:29). And that is exactly who He is, the Lamb whose blood was shed so that we might obtain forgiveness for our sins—forever.

When Christ died and rose again, the requirements of the ceremonial laws were canceled. There is no longer a need for animal sacrifices or the other ceremonial components of the law. We are saved, we are forgiven, we are purified, through the blood of Christ.

Moral Laws

Third, there were the moral laws, embodied in the Ten Commandments. These laws represent God's moral character, and His moral character does not change—ever.

Is it not a bit ridiculous to think that 3,500 years ago God was opposed to stealing, but now He has changed His mind? Is it not ludicrous to say that adultery offended Him then, but it is of little importance to Him now?

Yet this is exactly what some people think. They view God as having mellowed over the years—like a parent who was more strict with his oldest children, but then lets his last-born get away with everything. But God is consistent. He is fair. His character is firm forever. He is the same today as He was 3,500 years ago—just as He will be the same four million years into the future.

Thus, we find frequent references to God's moral laws in the

New Testament as well as the Old. And when Paul gives a wonderful summation of the Christian Gospel, he ends by writing, "Do we then make void the law through faith? Certainly not! On the contrary, we establish the law" (Romans 3:31).

The Old Testament Scriptures promised that the commandments of God—His law—would one day be written upon the fleshly tablets of human hearts. And now they are. For the Christian, who has been saved by faith alone, each facet, each commandment, answers some aspect of the great question: How can I behave in a way that glorifies and pleases God and allows me to live the best life possible on this earth?

THE BALANCE BETWEEN GRACE AND LAW

The word "law" in Greek is *nomos,* and those who say that the law has no place at all in the Christian life are called antinomians, which means "against the law." Ever since the first century, some people have said, "We are saved by grace through faith, so we are free to do whatever we want." Interestingly, the first heresy trial conducted in America was for the heresy of antinomianism.

Whenever I encounter people who hold this view—and there have been quite a few—I always ask, "Having accepted Christ and been saved by His grace, is it not your desire to please Christ and to show your love to Him out of gratitude?"

"Oh, absolutely," they answer.

My next question is: "Can you name one thing you could do that would please God more than obeying His commandments?"

That question is always met with silence.

There is nothing that would please Him more. He doesn't want us inventing ways to please Him. Like most fathers, He wants us to show our love by respecting Him and living in obedience to His commandments. In the Old Testament, God makes it very clear that He does not want us inventing activities to please Him, when He says, "Who has required this from your hand, to trample My courts?" (Isaiah 1:12). In other words, "Who told you it was all right to walk all over My righteous decrees and scorn My laws?"

We who love the Lord, who are saved by grace through faith in Christ alone, desire to please Him in everything we do. For us, the moral laws of God—His Ten Commandments—serve as a guide, showing us how we can demonstrate our love and gratitude for Jesus Christ.

Admittedly, some people obey God because they are afraid of what He will do to them if they don't! They fear His wrath and punishment. They see themselves winding up as derelicts or unhappily divorced people chasing after meaningless sexual encounters. They are terrified of becoming the empty modern man, for whom nothing is absolute, sacred, or meaningful.

But that is not the right motivation for keeping God's commandments.

We do not obey out of fear, like slaves who avoid the sting of the taskmaster's whip. We obey because we are children of a loving Father, and we want to please Him. We should strive to be like King David, who said, "Oh, how I love Your law! It is my meditation all the day" (Psalms 119:97).

CHOOSE MERCY OVER JUSTICE

As we begin our study of the Ten Commandments, let me assure you that your obedience to God's laws has nothing at all to do with obtaining, earning, or meriting salvation. But I also hasten to assure you that obedience is the way you express your gratitude for salvation.

I have heard it said that the teachings of most of the world's religions can be summed up in one small word: "Do." "Do this and do that, and perhaps God (or the gods) will be merciful to you."

Only Christianity says, "Done!" The last words of Christ on the cross were: "It is finished!" (John 19:30). In Greek the expression is *tetelestai*! "It is accomplished!" Christ has paid it all.

There is nothing you can do to attain salvation because Christ has already done it all. As Dr. William Culbertson, Moody Bible Institute's president from 1948 to 1971, put it, "Every pagan religion in the world sings this hymn: 'Something in my hands I bring.' Only Christianity says, 'Nothing in my hands I bring. Only to the Cross I cling.' "

The only thing that remains for you to do is to accept by His grace what Christ has done for you—the salvation He offers you.

Salvation, you see, is by grace and grace alone. Almighty God has given His Son to endure the requirements of justice, to pay the legislated penalty, to suffer infinitely in our stead. And now all those who come to God empty-handed, abandoning all trust in their own goodness and clinging to Christ's Cross, will be granted mercy.

You may stand before God, having violated every commandment, worthy of nothing but condemnation. But if, like the dying thief on the cross, you place your faith in Christ, you will be granted everlasting life in His kingdom. You will be adopted into His family, allowed to take His name, given a place in His will, and permitted entrance into Paradise. That is the wonder of grace.

Have you accepted the saving grace Christ offers you? If not, I urge you to take a few moments to receive Christ and His pardon right now. Wherever you may be, stop and pray this prayer with me:

O God, I know that I am a sinner. I know that I have no hope of eternal life except through the blood of Your only Son, Jesus Christ, who gave His life for me so that I may live eternally. Lord Jesus, cleanse me of my sinfulness. I open my heart and life to be pleasing to You. Thank You for the promise of eternal life, which even now I possess. I ask this in Your precious name. Amen.

If you just prayed that prayer, or if you had already accepted Christ as your Lord and Savior, you have stepped out of the realm of guilt and condemnation and into the realm of mercy.

If you are a Christian already, may this be your prayer today:

Father, even though I am Your child, I cannot protest my innocence to You. I have broken Your moral law, and I have sinned—not only against You but against others as well.

But I long to show You my gratitude for dying for me. I long to live in ways that are pleasing in Your sight, and witness to others of the life that is good.

Teach me, Father, where I am living outside Your law. Correct me, Father, and help me to become Your obedient child. To Your glory and honor. Amen.

CHAPTER TWO

The One True God

So it was that the children of Israel had sinned against the LORD their God, who had brought them up out of the land of Egypt, from under the hand of Pharaoh king of Egypt; and they had feared other gods. . . .

Therefore the LORD was very angry with Israel, and removed them from His sight; there was none left but the tribe of Judah alone.

—2 KINGS 17:7, 18

SOME YEARS AGO, a group of seminary students was given an assignment to rearrange the Ten Commandments in order of priority. They were instructed to begin with the most important commandment and end with the one they considered to be the least important.

Pens began scratching away as each student attacked the project with enthusiasm. When everyone was finished, the lists were compiled into one master list. The majority of students concluded that the most important commandment is "you shall not murder." After that came "you shall not steal." Next on the list was "you shall not bear false witness," and so on.

At the very end of the list there was a toss-up. Half of the class felt the least important commandment was "you shall not commit adultery." (Apparently, prohibitions against sexual sin were not such a big deal to these students.) The other choice for last place was "you shall have no other gods before Me." The tie was finally broken when, after some discussion, the class decided that not putting other "gods" first was the least important of the Ten Commandments.

God, who is infinitely wise, has another idea! There is no question about which commandment is most important to Him. After all, He wrote the list, and first in His order of importance is "you shall have no other gods before Me."

Years ago, the great theologian Dr. Charles Hodge, of Princeton University, wrote, "The duty to which we are directed by this commandment is the highest duty of man." Christ obviously agreed with this assessment. When He was asked, "Which is the great commandment in the law?" He answered, " 'You shall love the LORD your God with all your heart, with all your soul, and with all your mind.' This is the first and great commandment" (Matthew 22:36-38).

God demands first place in our lives, and it is only right that He should do so. He is the Author of our being, the One on whom we are absolutely dependent, the rightful Possessor of our souls and bodies. He is God, the Creator of everything we see, and those He created must worship and revere Him. I believe that we find peace and fulfillment only when we give God His rightful place in our lives.

Consider, for example, the Russian novelist and philosopher Leo Tolstoy. He was wealthy beyond the dreams of even the most avaricious man, and he was honored and acclaimed for his writing throughout the world. He was also exceptionally sinful and bragged about it. But with all of his wealth and fame, discontent gnawed at him.

One day he was walking in the countryside and came upon a peasant who had a look of peace, quiet, and contentment on his face. Tolstoy realized immediately that the man had virtually nothing of his own, and yet his face beamed with the joy of living.

For days and weeks the wealthy and celebrated Tolstoy could not get that radiant peasant out of his mind. After much agonizing, he concluded that the difference between himself and the peasant was that the poor man knew God, while he did not. Thus began the journey that ultimately led Tolstoy to Christ—the answer to the discontent that had always plagued him. Tolstoy later said, "To know God and to live is one and the same thing. God is life." How true that is.

Tolstoy learned, as have many others before and since, that the fall of man is nothing other than a steep plunge away from a relationship with God. And without a relationship with God, we are dead.

Patrick Henry, the statesman and hero of the American Revolution, is remembered for the stirring speech in which he cried out, "Give me liberty or give me death!" When this patriot wrote his last will and testament, he presented his children with the substance of true wealth: "This is all the inheritance I can give to my dear family. The religion of Christ can give them one which will make them rich indeed."

Henry was speaking of nothing else but our first duty, and the soul's first need, which is to place God first and above all else in our lives. Those who crowd God out of His rightful place in their lives do so to their detriment. If the one true God is not on the throne in your life, you will never know true happiness.

C. S. Lewis said, "We are half-hearted creatures, fooling about with drink and sex and ambition, when infinite joy is offered us, like an ignorant child who wants to keep on making mud pies in a slum because he cannot imagine what is meant by the offer of a holiday at the sea. We are far too easily pleased."[1]

"HEAR, O ISRAEL: THE LORD OUR GOD, THE LORD IS ONE"

Perhaps one of the most profound things that happened on Mount Sinai was that God introduced Himself to the children of Israel. Prior to that, He had met their fathers, Abraham, Isaac, and Jacob. Just prior to the Exodus, He had met face-to-face with Moses. He had been their God. Now, to the whole house of Jacob—Israel—He said, "I am the LORD your God."

It is amazing how much can be revealed by a simple little word such as "I." This little pronoun, only one letter long, conveys a profound and fundamental truth about who God is. In identifying Himself with this word, He demonstrates the error that exists in several age-old forms of religious thinking, forms that are making a popular comeback. When He said, "I am the LORD," He effectively destroyed pantheism, polytheism, deism, and New Age thinking. Let's take a closer look at each of these beliefs, beginning with:

Pantheism

When God said, "I AM" (Exodus 3:14), He revealed that He is a person. He was saying, in essence, "I think. I feel. I act." God is not, as pantheism teaches, an impersonal force. Pantheism is the old religious theory that teaches that all (*pan*) is God (*theos*). The universe is God. Everything is God. One believer in this religion was asked, "Do you believe that the devil is God?" And he answered, "Of course. Who doubts it?" Pantheism is the worst form of religion. Why? Because if all is God, there can be no distinction between good and evil.

Christian Science, which is simply a Westernized form of Buddhism, reasons this way: "God is good. God is all. All is good." Therefore, according to this logic, if a drunk driver runs a red light, slams into your car, and one of your children is injured or killed, you must conclude that this is good. Pain and harm and death do not matter. The pantheist believes that what the drunk driver has done is no different from the actions of someone like Florence Nightingale, the heroine who ministered to the sick and injured during the Crimean War.

Polytheism

When God called Himself "I," He also exposed the lie inherent in a form of religious thought known as polytheism. Polytheists believe in many gods. But God didn't say, "We are the lords your gods." He said, "I am the Lord your God." He is One and One only. There are no other gods.

In fact, the apostle Paul tells us that those who worship the so-called gods of the pagan world are bowing before demons in disguise (1 Corinthians 10:20).

Deism

In expressing His desire for a personal relationship with the Israelites, God destroyed the notion of deism, which is not nearly as popular at this particular moment in history as it was a few centuries ago. Deism might be considered the religion of the "clockmaker" God. Deism proposes that God created the world, wound it up like a clock, and then went off and forgot all about it. According to this way of thinking, God has no interest in the world. There's no use in praying to Him because He's not listening. His phone is off the hook.

That is most definitely not the God we encounter in the book of Exodus—the God who heard the cries of the children of Israel in their bondage and, with a mighty arm, freed them from Pharaoh, brought them across the sea and the desert, and led them to the foot of Mount Sinai. No, deism cannot be true. There is too much evidence all around us that God is very much involved in our world.

The late Dr. Francis Schaeffer said that the God of the Bible is the infinite personal God. Schaeffer wrote in *The God Who Is There:*

> The gods of the East are infinite by definition—the definition being "god is all that is." This is the pan-everything-ism god. The gods of the West tended to be personal but limited; such were the gods of the Greeks, Romans, and Germans. But the God of the Bible, Old and New Testaments alike, is the infinite-personal God.[2]

New Age Religion

God's statement on the mountain also ruled out New Age theology, which is very simplistic. It says, "Do you want to find God? Then look in the mirror." In other words, you are God, and so am I! I doubt if any of the Israelites believed that. Especially not when the mountain was quaking, the ground was shaking, and the voice of God was so terrifying that the people feared for their lives. I doubt very much that anyone stood up at that time and said, "Wait a minute, Voice. You have this all wrong. I'm god. So be quiet. Listen to me."

This New Age thinking is nothing but the old lie of the devil, the one he told Eve in the Garden of Eden: "You will be like God" (Genesis 3:5).

Anyone who is under the assumption that man is God must not be reading the newspaper or watching the evening news. Man is often cruel, violent, self-centered, and greedy. God, on the other hand, is kind, peaceful, loving, and giving. As we read in Exodus:

> The Lord, the Lord God, merciful and gracious, longsuffering, and abounding in goodness and truth, keeping mercy for thousands, forgiving iniquity and transgressions and sin, by no means clearing the guilty, visiting the iniquity of the fathers upon the children and the children's children to the third and the fourth generation (34:6-7).

I believe that man was created in God's image, as the Bible says, but God is in heaven and not within fallen man.

I have been amazed lately to see that no matter how vile and perverted a person's conduct may be, he will continue to insist that he is basically a good person.

In the news recently, there was a story about a young man who robbed another young man and then shot him in the head. He was arrested, and during his first court appearance, he flew into such a rage that it took four policemen to subdue him. What was the source of his anger? He didn't want people to think ill of him. He didn't want them to think of him as a monster. He wanted everyone to know that the shooting really wasn't his fault. He killed the other fellow only because the guy touched him.

Are you catching this? He killed a man for no reason at all. And yet he wants the world to believe that he's basically a "good guy." So much for the New Age belief in "the God within."

GLIMPSING THE CHARACTER OF GOD

Just as we can learn something of the character of man by reading the daily newspaper, we can see two important components of God's character in the events leading up to the giving of the Ten Commandments. In the first commandment, we learn that God is:

Gracious

Some people claim that they cannot find any grace in the God of the Old Testament, and yet this very first of the Ten Commandments is full of grace: "I am the Lord your God, who brought you out of the land of Egypt, out of the house of bondage" (Exodus 20:2). There is grace. First, He redeemed them—not because of anything they did—because He is a God of mercy and love. He showed them, through His actions, that He is worthy of their worship. Now He wants them to know that He alone is God.

Think of everything God went through to bring the Israelites out of captivity in Egypt. First, He appeared to Moses in the burning bush and told him to go to Pharaoh and say, "Let my people go." As you probably know, Moses didn't want the job. In fact, he tried to get the Lord to send someone else. "O my Lord," he said, "I am not eloquent, neither before nor since You have spoken to Your servant; but I am slow of speech and slow of tongue" (Exodus 4:10).

Finally, reluctantly, Moses agreed that he would appear before Pharaoh, as the Lord had commanded him. But even though God performed miracle after miracle, Pharaoh refused to release the Israelite slaves. Our gracious God expended His supernatural power to bring freedom to people who, for the most part, would not appreciate it in the least.

Why did God go to all this trouble? Because of His grace and mercy. As He said to Moses, "I have surely seen the oppression of My people who are in Egypt, and have heard their cry because of their taskmasters, for I know their sorrows. So I have come down to deliver them out of the hand of the Egyptians" (Exodus 3:7-8).

As He led the Israelites through the wilderness, God continued to be gracious toward them. He fed them manna and quail. He gave them water to drink. He saw to it that their clothes did not wear out. He protected them from their enemies. And how did they repay Him? They grumbled and whined and insisted they had been better off as slaves. Even so, God did not abandon them. Now, that's grace!

Jealous

As He commanded the Israelites to make Him first in their lives, God also told them that He is "a jealous God" (Exodus 20:5). For most of us, that word "jealous" has only negative connotations.

We think immediately of a jealous lover, who is controlling and demanding, and flies into a rage without the slightest reason.

But what God was revealing about Himself here is something quite the opposite of the small-minded, mean little tyrant. He was showing the Israelites that within Him burns the jealousy of the loving parent who sees beauty, possibility, and value in a son or daughter, and who is brokenhearted to see a child wasting all of these gifts.

Some children just won't listen to their parents. They don't trust their parents' experience and want to learn things for themselves—often with dire consequences. Sadly, some children continue their whole lives in rebellion to the wisdom and guidance of their parents, and never learn at all.

God does not want us to be like that! He knows what is best for His children. And He watches jealously, desiring that we become the best people we can be, that we develop all of the potential He has placed within us—the potential to become the obedient sons and daughters of the living God.

God does not want us to waste ourselves on the worship of false gods. He is the only One who has just claim to our lives because He created us, and He is the only One who can tell us how to live in the best way possible.

WHO IS ON THE THRONE OF YOUR LIFE?

Now some of us may feel pretty smug when we read the first commandment. We may think, *I'm not tempted to worship other gods. I certainly don't believe in Baal or Ashteroth. And I'm not about to convert to Islam or Buddhism.*

But, you see, these are not the only types of false gods. Anything that crowds God out of His rightful place in your life is a false god.

Is your job more important to you than God? Then you are in direct disobedience to the first commandment. Would you rather go fishing or play softball than worship the Lord with your fellow Christians on Sunday morning? Then you, too, are violating the first commandment. Whatever is most important in your life is your god.

Does your family mean more to you than God? Is your husband first in your life? Or do you spend more time thinking about your children than you do thinking about God or meditating on His Word?

Do not misunderstand me. I am not saying that your family or your job should not be important to you. But I am saying that God must be most important. If, after an honest examination, you realize that God does not have first place in your life, it is time to reorder your priorities and begin living the way He commands you to live.

There was a time, before I came to know the grace of God in Jesus Christ, when God was not in many of my thoughts. I had my own agenda. I had my own plans. I had my own advancement in mind. I had things I wanted to do, and God had nothing to do with them. That's how millions of people live out their lives.

"They never think of Him," says Princeton's Dr. Hodge. "They do not recognize His providence. They do not refer to His will as a rule of conduct. They do not feel their responsibility to Him for what they think or do. They do not worship Him, nor thank Him for His mercies. They are without God in the world. Yet [and this is stunning] they think well of themselves."[3]

How would they feel about someone who was brought into the world by loving parents, cared for and fed from infancy on up, provided the finest of everything from his very first day—and then, as soon as he reached adulthood, turned his back on his parents? He never comes to visit; he never calls; he never writes. He has nothing to do with them. As Shakespeare wrote, "How sharper than a serpent's tooth it is to have a thankless child." It's hard to imagine someone being that wicked and ungrateful, isn't it? But millions and millions treat their heavenly Father exactly that way.

If you have not, by grace, made God the Lord of your life—as we discussed in chapter 1—then His commandments are bound to be galling and hateful to you. You despise them and want to get as far away from them as you possibly can. But if you are in a right relationship with Him—the filial relationship of child to Father—His will is your delight. What you want to do most is please Him. In other words, your attitude toward the law reveals your attitude toward God, and whether you relate to Him as a cold, harsh taskmaster or as a loving Father.

JESUS IS JEHOVAH

Perhaps you're beginning to realize that we human beings need help. We need forgiveness. We need the grace of God. That is why this great God—Jehovah—who spoke with a thunderous voice at Sinai came into this world in the person of Jesus Christ. Because we desperately needed His rescuing grace, He mounted a smaller hill outside the city wall surrounding Jerusalem. And there He hung on the Cross, agonizing in our place, paying for our heinous transgressions. There He opened His arms wide to receive us back unto Himself, that we may love and obey Him as we were created to do.

Am I saying that Jesus of Nazareth—who died, was crucified, and rose again—is the same person as the God who gave the Ten Commandments? Exactly.

If you are reading the King James or New King James Version of the Bible, you will notice that the word "Lord" is usually printed in capital letters in the Old Testament. That means it is the translation of the Hebrew word *Yahweh*, which was eventually translated into English as "Jehovah." But Jehovah is the name of the triune God—Jehovah the Father, Jehovah the Son, Jehovah the Holy Spirit. Three distinct persons, all fully God, who make up the holy Trinity.

Lacing together the Old and New Testaments, there are many of what scholars refer to as "Jehovah-Jesus passages." These texts from the Old Testament talk about Jehovah, echoed by texts in the New Testament referring to Jesus Christ. For example, God told the prophet Isaiah, "I am the First and I am the Last" (Isaiah 44:6). And Jesus said in the book of Revelation, "I am . . . the First and the Last" (22:13). There can be only one first and one last, and that is Jehovah. In this case, it is Jehovah Jesus. Here are some other similar passages:

The psalmist said, "The Lord is my shepherd" (Psalms 23:1). The Lord Jehovah is my Shepherd. Jesus said, "I am the good shepherd" (John 10:11).

The psalmist wrote, "Bless the LORD, O my soul . . . who forgives all your iniquities" (Psalms 103:2-3). Jesus said, "The Son of Man has power on earth to forgive sins" (Matthew 9:6).

In Exodus, when God first revealed His name to Moses, He said, "I AM WHO I AM." He also told Moses to tell the Israelites that "I AM" had sent him to rescue them (Exodus 3:14). Jesus repeated that statement when He said, "Before Abraham was, I AM" (John 8:58).

As we can see from these passages, Jesus and Jehovah are One.

Just as Jehovah the Father redeemed the Israelites from the house of bondage and led them safely out of Egypt, Jesus has redeemed us from bondage to sin and redeemed us from its curse, which is eternal punishment and separation from God. He brought us the help we so desperately needed, and He did it by shedding His blood on the Cross of Calvary.

It comes to this: Jesus became the one and only Bridge Builder between God and man. He was and is the only Redeemer of mankind. But the redemption He brought will do you no good as an individual unless and until, by God's grace, you accept it. The bridge He built won't be of any benefit to you unless you walk across it.

All of my life, as far back as I can remember, I believed in God and knew that Jesus was the Savior of the world. Yet for many years Jesus was not my Savior. The day that, by grace, I acknowledged my sinful condition before God and accepted Jesus' shed blood as my only hope, I crossed the only bridge open to us as men and entered the new covenant offered by God Himself. I was converted.

Today there are many people who believe in God, but He is not their God. They have no relationship with Him. They don't trust Him; they trust in themselves. Insofar as we trust in ourselves, we scorn God's sacrifice for our sins, and we do not love Him. We live outside the covenant relationship with Him.

How about you? Have you entered into the life-transforming relationship that is offered to you through the blood of Jesus? If so, have you recognized the false gods that demand your time, attention, and service? Have you turned away from them and their demands to revere and serve the one true God alone? Does He have first place in your life?

Do money or possessions come before Him in your priorities? Does your plan for your life come before anything He might want for you? Do you choose family over your heavenly Father? Yes, God demands first place in your heart, even before your parents, spouse, and children.

Are you trusting in God and God alone? Some people put their trust in people. Others in their financial investments. Some put their trust in their reputation or the family they were born into. But all of these things will fail you. God and God alone is trustworthy.

As the old hymn proclaims, "On Christ the solid rock I stand, all other ground is sinking sand."

If you are standing on sinking sand right now, I urge you to step onto the solid rock by telling God that you will make Him first in your life from this day forward. You will be eternally glad you did.

Heavenly Father, I pray that if there are any reading these words who have not come to You and trusted You and received forgiveness, You will, by Your Holy Spirit, draw them now unto Yourself. Open their eyes that they may see not only their guilt, but also the glory of Your love and compassion and mercy, and they may say, "O blessed Savior, come into my life right now and forgive me for my sins. I am sorry for what I have done to You. Cleanse me and make me anew." In Your most holy name I pray. Amen.

CHAPTER THREE

False Gods

All the people broke off the golden earrings which were in their ears, and brought them to Aaron. And he received the gold from their hand, and he fashioned it with an engraving tool, and made a molded calf. Then they said, "This is your god, O Israel, that brought you out of the land of Egypt!"

. . . And the LORD *said to Moses, "Go, get down! For your people whom you brought out of the land of Egypt have corrupted themselves. They have turned aside quickly out of the way which I commanded them. They have made themselves a molded calf, and worshiped it and sacrificed to it, and said, 'This is your god, O Israel, that brought you out of the land of Egypt!'" And the* LORD *said to Moses, "I have seen this people, and indeed it is a stiff-necked people! Now therefore, let Me alone, that My wrath may burn hot against them and I may consume them."*

—EXODUS 32:3-4, 7-10

You shall not make for yourself a carved image—any likeness of anything that is in heaven above, or that is in the earth beneath, or that is in the water under the earth; you shall not bow down to them nor serve them.

—EXODUS 20:4-5

HOW WOULD YOU respond if your best friend took you aside and confronted you with the suggestion that you are guilty of idolatry? Would you be indignant, perhaps even outraged?

I imagine that most people reading this book today would consider the prohibition of idol worship to be the most outdated of God's Ten Commandments. We tend to think of idolatry as a practice that was prominent in pagan cultures thousands of years ago.

But today, and surely in the Christianized West, idolatry is no longer a problem . . . or is it? I believe if we examine our society closely, we are forced to admit that we have our own false gods, even today. Far from being outdated, God's prohibition of idolatry still applies to us.

WHEN GOD REPEATS HIMSELF, HE MEANS BUSINESS

The commandment against idolatry is the most repeated commandment of all. In fact, there are more denunciations of idolatry than any other sin. If you own a good Bible concordance, I encourage you to look up this subject and read through some of the hundreds of references you will find listed under key words such as "idolatry," "idols," "idolaters," and "idolatrous." God's voice speaks loudly and clearly against the sin of idolatry throughout Old and New Testament Scriptures. Listen now to just a few of His pronouncements on this subject:

> Do not turn to idols, nor make for yourselves molded gods: I am the LORD your God (Leviticus 19:4).

> Thus saith the Lord GOD; Repent, and turn yourselves from your idols; and turn away your faces from all your abominations. For every one . . . which setteth up his idols in his heart . . . I the LORD will answer him by myself (Ezekiel 14:6-7, KJV).

> The works of the flesh are evident, which are: adultery, fornication, uncleanness, lewdness, idolatry, sorcery, hatred, contentions, jealousies, outbursts of wrath, selfish ambitions, dissensions, heresies, envy, murders, drunkenness, revelries, and the like . . . those who practice such things will not inherit the kingdom of God (Galatians 5:19-21).

> Little children, keep yourselves from idols (1 John 5:21).

From these select few passages of Scripture alone, it would appear that God knows something about the human heart that we do not know—or perhaps it is something we stubbornly resist knowing. It is that the sin of idolatry runs deep, cutting into the human psyche. Prophets, apostles, and preachers down through the centuries have recognized that there is a tendency in the human heart—a stream that flows dangerously in the cold caverns of the fallen soul—to worship things other than God.

The commandment against idol worship was broken before the words burned in the tablets of stone by the finger of the Almighty even cooled. The Israelites had already fashioned a graven image of a golden calf. They had risen up to worship the idol right beneath the gaze of Jehovah.

How could God's chosen people have bowed down before a cold, lifeless image of a calf when they had just seen the great God Jehovah smite down the gods of Egypt? How could they be so unfaithful to the Holy One who brought them out of captivity on eagle's wings—the One who led them across the Red Sea, where the waters stood up like pillars on either side? How could they have possibly worshiped a golden calf when they personally knew the living, breathing, almighty God?

Look closely at the biblical account of this event, and you will begin to understand why idolatry is so offensive to God. Note Aaron's response in Exodus 32:22-24, when he was confronted about this abomination. He made a feeble claim that they did nothing wrong saying that he threw all the gold in the fire . . . and out came the calf. Aaron had earlier told the people that the feast they held was a feast to Jehovah, not to the calf (Exodus 32:5). In other words, as they ate and bowed down to the golden statue, they were worshiping Jehovah through the calf. He emphatically claimed they were not worshiping the calf. But the Bible makes it abundantly clear that idolatry is not just the worshiping of images or pictures or statues. It is equally idolatrous to use an image of any sort as a "vessel" to worship the one true God.

SIN UPON SIN

The pages of the Bible are filled with accounts of how the Israelites piled sin upon sin as they repeatedly disobeyed the second commandment. Many years after Aaron's generation fashioned the first golden calf, Jeroboam repeated the sin of his forefathers (1 Kings 12:25-31) by creating another golden calf in Dan, and yet another in Bethel! Despite the commandment prohibiting idol worship, the people once again bowed down to lifeless objects of worship. All over Israel, on every hill and in every clump of trees, altars were created bearing the images of false gods. On and on went the idolatry until, at long length, the patience of God was exhausted.

To chastise the Israelites, He providentially allowed the hordes of Babylon, under Nebuchadnezzar, to sweep across the plains of Israel. The walls of Jerusalem were torn down, and the people were led off into captivity. Sadly, it took the soul-cleansing furnace of slavery in Babylon to burn the dredges of idolatry from the hearts of the people. When their hearts were purified, God moved again to bring them back to their home—the promised land of Israel—and to the worship of the one true God.

EXCLUSIVITY

At this point, let's stop and make sure we understand what the first two commandments are really teaching. The first commandment was "thou shalt have no other gods before me" (Exodus 20:3 KJV). It compels us to worship the God of Abraham, Isaac, and Jacob. Exclusively. Christianity is not pluralistic. Christianity carries on the tradition of exclusivity. Neither the Old nor the New Testament writers were tolerant of other gods because God Almighty is not tolerant of other deities. That is a point about which the Bible is unambiguous and unequivocal from cover to cover. In 1 Corinthians 10:20, the apostle Paul emphasized that all of the other gods and all of their images are simply demons. He emphatically charged his readers not to have fellowship with demons.

The second commandment calls us to worship God spiritually—not with carnal or material outward forms and offerings. Jesus told the woman at the well in Samaria, "God is Spirit, and those who worship Him must worship in spirit and truth" (John 4:24). He was telling her that God does not want our worship to be an empty form or ritual. He wants us to know, love, and honor Him from the heart, according to His revealed truth.

Furthermore, the second commandment is obviously of great importance because it is the only commandment where God says that those who break it hate Him. If you worship a false god or any sort of image, or even if you attempt to worship the true God through some kind of visible, tangible aid, then you hate God. That's not my opinion; it is what God says. He is very clear that He is extremely grieved when people disobey this commandment.

A SOBER WARNING

Have you ever confronted someone about an action you know is wrong and heard him reply that he wasn't hurting anyone else, so why should you be concerned? Somehow that excuse justifies his actions in his own mind.

The problem is that our actions affect other people, and in the case of the second commandment, God says disobedience has serious repercussions for future generations, "visiting the iniquity of the fathers upon the children to the third and fourth generations of those who hate Me" (Exodus 20:5). I don't think that is something I want to mess around with. Do you? Obviously, it is a very serious sin—the worship of idols, images, or other false gods. Whether you call it worship or adoring or venerating or whatever term you choose, it is the same in the sight of God. His Word is clear: We are not to worship anything else in that way.

WHAT GOD IS NOT FORBIDDING

Some people suppose that this commandment altogether forbids the use of visual arts. It is easy to see how they could conclude that this is what the commandment forbids. Notice what God says: "You shall not make for yourself a carved image—any likeness of anything that is in heaven above, or that is in the earth beneath, or that is in the water under the earth" (Exodus 20:4).

That just about covers it all, doesn't it? Paintings and pictures and statues and representations and photographs and television and motion pictures and any other kinds of visual art are condemned. But people who make that claim don't read the passage in its totality and its context because it goes on to say, "You shall not bow down to them nor serve them."

Throughout Christian history there have been revival movements that have had an iconoclastic character to them. That is, people have taken this commandment so literally they've risen up in mobs and charged into cathedrals and churches, smashing frescoes and other works of legitimate art depicting sacred scenes.

The second commandment forbids idolatry. "Idolatry" comes from two Greek words: *eidolon* and *latria*. It means the service or worship of an idol. It can also mean the worship of the true God through an idol. But it is not sacred artistry that God forbids or condemns. It is the worship of anything in place of God.

Again, some very pious people have argued for absolute starkness in our sanctuaries and worship. But if we're not careful, we will miss the real point of the second commandment. It isn't a prohibition against artistry and beauty, because on the same day that God gave Moses these commandments, He gave Moses all of the instructions for the building of the tabernacle. In that tabernacle there were to be all manner of visual arts. You can find a detailed description of God's specifications for the tabernacle in chapters 25 and 26 of the book of Exodus. On the veil that separated the holy place from the Holy of Holies were depicted flowers, pomegranates, palm trees, and many other beautiful things. The ark that God asked Moses to build was to be overlaid with pure gold, with a carved cherub on each end.

Later on in history, the details that God gave Solomon about the building of the temple were even more elaborate. Obviously, there is a distinction between idols as objects of worship and sacred artistry that is pleasing to God. He did not have an attack of forgetfulness and violate His own law! You may argue that when He defines graven images, God is really talking about statues and other three-dimensional kinds of art. That allegation won't stand up either. If you happened to be the high priest, on the annual high Day of Atonement you would pass through the veil that leads from the holy place into the Holy of Holies. There, and in that most silent place, you would find the ark of the covenant. Inside that ark were the rod of Moses, a pot of manna, and the two tablets of the Law. On the top was the golden mercy seat, and over the mercy seat there was a visible appearance of the glory of God—the Shekinah glory of God! Upon that mercy seat the priest sprinkled the blood once a year. The broken Law . . . the shattered tablets cried out to God for justice against those who had violated them, and it was the blood that protected the people from certain death.

On either side of the Shekinah glory were full-sized, three-dimensional figures depicting beings that are in Heaven above and sometimes on earth beneath. There were two cherubim or two angels with wings outspread until the tip of the wings touched the tent on either side of the Holy of Holies—one on each side of the ark of the covenant. In between, the glory of God Jehovah blazed every moment, day and night.

Did God forget that He had commanded them not to create any three-dimensional figures? Of course not. What God forbade was idolatry, the service or worship of an idol—or even of the true God through an idol.

THREE FUNCTIONS OF ART

Then, what shall we say is allowed and disallowed in this? I remember Dr. William Childs Robinson at Columbia Seminary pointed out that there are three uses of art:

Used for Decoration

There is, first of all, the decorative use of art, which fills most of our homes. Many devout women wear decorative jewelry that is a form of sacred art. Even our churches are decorated with art. These objects of art are not objects of worship. Therefore, they are obviously not condemned. God is a God of beauty. He changed the chaos into the cosmos—a beautiful creation. The very word "cosmos" means order and beauty. God is the great Artist who gilds our mornings with golden sunrises and paints the evening sky with magnificent sunsets. He sculpts the glory of the budding flowers, the beautiful trees and plants we enjoy. God is not opposed to art. Edith Schaeffer, in her book *Hidden Art*, reminds us that those who have been recreated in Jesus Christ in the image of God are to work with Him as creators of beauty.[1] We should exercise our God-given talents to beautify this world.

Art Used as God's Teaching Tool

Second, there is the didactic use of art, which means that God uses art to teach us many things. The Chinese proverb says that one picture is worth a thousand words. Hundreds of millions of children down through the ages fondly remember learning about the acts of God through pictures—pictures of Noah going up the ramp into the ark with the animals, illustrations of Adam and Eve in the Garden, vibrant scenes of David slaying Goliath and Samson killing the lion with his strong bare hands. Pictures of all kinds of Bible stories are used to teach great truths—Jesus with the lamb, the lost sheep upon His bosom, and many others—particularly pictures of Christ dying upon a Cross for our sins. Yes, all of these are marvelous teaching tools in God's hands that have been used to press into the minds and hearts of people the stories of the Bible.

Art Used for Devotional Purpose

The third use of art—and the only one God condemns—is the devotional use of art. For example, someone bows before a picture or a statue or any kind of representation of anything in Heaven or on earth, especially the things that supposedly represent God. Of course, one reason we should have no such representation of God is that all are distortions of God. Do you think Jehovah God looked like a cow? That is absurd! Have you ever looked at a picture and been astounded that it is absolutely the worst picture anyone has ever taken of you? If the photographer had good sense, the picture would have been torn up and never been shown to you or anybody else. But there you are, distorted and twisted. The image of you is all wrong. Your lovely self doesn't show through. We have all had that experience, I'm sure. And we don't find it amusing! Neither does God when vastly, infinitely worse distortions of His glory are made by people who arrogantly attempt to draw a picture of Him. As one of the early Church fathers wrote, in his appeal to pagan idolaters:

> All of nature, and any thing created by man, through which we can understand something of God's invisible attributes. Nothing that is made, or can be made, can represent the full glory of our unseen and eternal God. For He Himself is greater than His creation and everything in it. And so to bow down to any created thing is a great evil.[2]

THE LORD IS A JEALOUS GOD

Why is God so opposed to the devotional use of art to represent Himself? First, of course, is the sin of worshiping something other than God Himself, to whom alone all glory and reverence is due. But there is another reason. He is jealous for our good in the same ways that every father is "jealous" for his children. For example, a caring father is "jealous" (and thus zealous) that his children might have the best education, that they might eat the best food, that they might have the best care, that they might grow up to be the best people they possibly can be. A caring father is angry with anything that threatens the best for his children—anything that might harm them in any way.

God has this kind of jealousy. It does not mean He is petty, strange, or violent—like a jealous spouse. Because God is always and only good, it is for our good when He is jealous. He wants to keep us close to Him and mold us into His image. Whether we are talking about pagan idols or those of modern Americans, they are always infinitely less than God. We don't make our idols today out of wood or gold. We don't carve statues and fall down before them in adoration. Such a practice seems insanely barbaric to us. Yet we do worship idols in other ways. Let me give you a few examples:

Janice is very proud of her home. She spends hours each day cleaning—vacuuming the carpet, dusting the furniture, scrubbing every square inch of grout in her bathroom tiles. It makes her feel good when visitors comment on what a beautiful home she has, but her kids resent her compulsive cleanliness. They never invite their friends to come over because Janice is so paranoid about their spilling a drink on the carpet or messing up things. Janice has distorted the home that God provided as a place of shelter and comfort for her family, and she has made it into a shrine unto itself. She spends far more time working on her house than she does on Bible study, prayer, or church activities.

Dan serves his athletic body. He works out in a gym five days a week and has impeccable eating habits. He is attracted only to other "beautiful body" people. The problem is that he keeps falling for shallow women who have no depth of spirit or character. A short time into a new relationship, he feels empty, lonely, disillusioned, burned out . . . and eventually, he becomes bored, bitter, and cynical. The false god of vanity fails him time and time again.

Debby's family means everything to her. Her son and daughter play sports, take music and art lessons, and attend the finest private school available. Debby spends every waking moment of every day taking care of her kids—driving them to school and extracurricular activities, making sure they eat right, hovering over them when they are sick. Debby's husband loves their kids, too, but frankly, he's grown jealous of them. His wife never has time for him. He feels that all he's good for is to bring home the money to pay for piano lessons, sports equipment, and school fees. If Debby's husband feels neglected, how does God feel? Of course, He wants Debby to take care of her family! But she has taken her responsibility to an extreme. She lives through her children; they are like false gods in her life.

These examples may be a bit exaggerated, but if you think about it, I'm sure you can think of people you know who fit one of these profiles. Many other subtle "gods" rule our lives. Money, success, fancy cars, prestige. Although we may not literally bow down to statues or carved idols, we certainly have progressive and modern practices of idolatry in our lives. We fashion them in the factories of our minds. We create our own gods.

I remember a conversation with a woman about how God is loving and kind, but also just and holy. I told her that God promises to visit our transgressions with His rod and our iniquity with stripes. God's Word teaches this (Psalms 89:32). He will punish our sin. The woman looked at me and said, "Oh, no . . . no. My god would never be so harsh. My god would not do that." She could not accept what I told her because she had chosen to believe only in the loving, compassionate attributes of God. She refused to acknowledge His justifiable hatred of sin. She would not accept His rightful role as Judge. I had to reply by telling her the truth—that her god would never do anything like that because her god does not exist, except in her mind. She had designed her own god, a figment of her imagination. She had made a god that fit her criteria. I went on to explain that the one true God and Creator of the heavens and the earth, the God of Abraham, Isaac, and Jacob, the Father of our Lord Jesus Christ is clear about His role as Judge. He has declared that we will be punished for our sins unless we repent and turn to Christ.

Like that woman, we are prone to conjure up our own gods. Our gods today may be the gods of fame, success, or financial gain. The bottom line is this: Anything more important to us than God is an idol.

So let me ask you: What is most important to you? What is your god, created subtly as an idol of your mind? Remember! God will have no other gods before Him.

A HUMAN DILEMMA

Having examined God's second commandment carefully, we have come up against a dilemma. We hunger after a god we can see . . . or touch . . . or hear. This is our nature as human beings. How is that hunger to be satisfied?

Michelangelo once heard of a block of marble so large that his friends, who were sculptors, feared to use it for a project. But Michelangelo purchased it. He built a shed around it in which he could work, and he allowed no one to enter. He didn't want anyone to see what he was doing. Finally, after weeks and months of indefatigable labor, of chipping and polishing, at last the day came when his masterpiece was complete. He tore the shed down and invited the public to look upon his great work: David.

Michelangelo saw something in the block of marble—an

image hidden from the eyes of lesser sculptors. It was almost as if the marvelous form he envisioned was concealed from others until the right man and the right time came along.

When the right time came along, out of an obscure little village in Judea, God brought forth One who was revealed as the Son of God. Jesus is not made after the image of God. Jesus is not made in the image of God. The Bible states that Jesus Christ is the image of the invisible God (Hebrews 1:3). As such, He satisfies our hunger to feel and touch and hear the one true God.

I once asked a man who he thought Jesus was, and he replied, "Oh, He's the greatest man who ever lived."

I said, "Anything more?"

He said, "Not that I can think of."

I said, "Let me tell you this. He is the almighty, eternal Creator of the galaxies; He is the everlasting, omniscient God Almighty."

Immediately, the man's eyes half-filled with tears, and he said to me, "I've never heard that before in my life, but I always thought that is the way it ought to be."

THE ONE TRUE GOD: IS HE YOUR GOD?

I want you to stop for a moment and think very carefully about your life. What do you feel it is in your life that gives you the feeling of ultimate power, security, provision, love, faith, or truth? Do you think wealth is the ultimate goal? Is a loving relationship your first priority? Are your children the passion of your life? All of these things are worthwhile, but they can become idols. If you don't put them in their proper perspective, in time you will take on the worst attributes of these "false" gods. You will end up being let down and disillusioned. Not one of your false gods—whatever they may be—has the seeds of eternal life in it.

In the second commandment, God teaches us that nothing must be more important in our lives than He is. If you have a false god in which you trust, abandon it right now. Abandon it by turning your heart to the one true God. You can do this only by receiving the gift of forgiveness and salvation offered by grace through faith in His Son, Jesus Christ.

We hear it said about someone who is very spiritual, "He is very much like God." We are told that God is exactly like Jesus. What an incredible revelation! In 2 Peter 1:16 we read, "We did not follow cunningly devised fables [or myths]," but, as John stated, that "which we have heard, which we have seen with our eyes, which we have looked upon, and our hands have handled" (1 John 1:1). Here is the only acceptable image of the invisible God—Jesus Christ, His divine Son.

Have you come to know Him? He is the One, the only One, who can satisfy that desire to see and hear and know the true God. He is the One who is willing to come into your heart to cleanse you and forgive you and give you eternal life. If you have never met God personally, you can meet Him today. If you are a Christian who has been lured away by the enemy, you can be restored and cleansed now. Wherever you are right now, use the following prayer as your guideline to make sure your heart is totally surrendered in worship and adoration of the one true God.

Heavenly Father, I admit to You and to myself that I am ruled by false gods. But I know that Jesus has taken the punishment I deserve and that because He has, I can be restored to You. I pray that Your Spirit will come alive in my heart and that You will grant me mercy. I've seen You hanging upon a Cross in my place for my sins. I've seen Your glorious, triumphant victory over death, Your rising from the tomb. Now come, I pray, and quicken my heart and grant me the free gift of eternal life, for this day I place my trust only in You—the one true God. In Your name. Amen.

CHAPTER FOUR

Reverence for the Name of God

[Jesus said,] "I say to you, every sin and blasphemy will be forgiven men, but the blasphemy against the Spirit will not be forgiven men. . . . I say to you that for every idle word men may speak, they will give account of it in the day of judgment. For by your words you will be justified, and by your words you will be condemned."

—MATTHEW 12:31, 36-37

You shall not take the name of the LORD your God in vain, for the LORD will not hold him guiltless who takes His name in vain.

—EXODUS 20:7

YOU HEAR IT in movies. You hear it on television and on the radio and in restaurants. Everywhere you go these days, God's name is used in vain.

In America, a country born out of trust in God, how could it come to pass that people have so little respect for His name? A man named Gordon Reid remembers exactly when and how this assault on God began. According to him, it was back in 1976. Before that time, profaning God's name was rarely heard on the airwaves. Then a friend of Mr. Reid—an executive in the television industry—informed him that a decision had been made to lower the barrier. It was a decision that would sink our society deep into the mire of depravity.

NO ONE TOOK A STAND

For the first time, TV shows were allowed to use God's name as an oath. The executive decision makers waited for the outcry—the response of the American people exclaiming, "We will not put up with that sort of thing!"

They waited and they waited and they waited and they waited.

The protests were negligible. As a nation, we were silent. Now we are literally bombarded by profanity—specifically the kind that assaults God's name—almost every time we turn on the television. We have been desensitized by the media to a form of evil that once was unthinkable to man and still is to God.

Of course, people working in media usually give two explanations for this practice. They are nothing more than rationalized excuses for blasphemy.

First, they might say, "Well, after all, movies are just fantasies. You know, you may see a murder on-screen, but nobody is really murdered. A bank robbery may be staged to look very authentic on television, but no banks really lose any money. People are kidnapped, but when you turn off the show, everybody is safe and sound at home." This is all true. When actors and actresses dramatize scenes like these, they are just make-believe. But when the script calls for profanity or blasphemy, the fantasy ends. On screen or in real life, if the name of God is taken in vain, blasphemy has been committed. The third commandment has been broken. This excuse does not wash! "The LORD will not hold him guiltless who takes His name in vain" (Exodus 20:7).

The second excuse often heard goes something like this: "Well, you see, we are just a reflection of reality. We're just acting out what people do every day." The sad thing is that this is true. The reality is that people talk this way. Every day. Everywhere. They reflect what is going on in the gutter, in bars, in jail cells, and in a few other undesirable places. Because we hear it everywhere, the vileness is gradually permeating our entire nation. The big guys who make decisions for the entertainment industry are not just reflecting reality. They are pushing their favorite kind of reality—the reality that appeals to their depraved minds.

I don't know about you, but it hurts and offends me to hear God's name used in vain. It's almost like a physical slap sometimes. We were silent when we should have spoken up, and as time has passed, the blasphemy no longer fazes us as a society anymore. More and more people are doing it. That does not make it right, however.

In the nineteenth century, the atheist philosopher Friedrich Nietzsche, whom I mentioned previously, talked about the death of God. He predicted that God would become meaningless to people. When it didn't happen, he said, "Well, it awaits the next century." When God's people do not speak up for Him and His eternal glory, something of God always dies in the here and now. He loses credibility because the men and women who profess to believe in Him come across as hypocrites, cowards, and frauds. Since we are God's representatives, how are unbelievers to know God as He really is if we don't reflect His nature credibly?

WHY BLASPHEMY IS CONDEMNED

Why did God give us the third commandment? What difference does it make whether people take His name in vain? A great deal! You see, God is holy and sovereign, and He deserves respect. This is the first reason He condemns blasphemy. There really needs to be no other.

However, there is a second reason that God condemns blasphemy. He is our Creator. He is the Giver of life. He has given us intelligent minds, perceptive eyes, and hearing ears. He has given each of us a mouth and enabled us to speak. And how should we use this tongue? The Westminster Shorter Catechism tells us, "The chief end of man is to glorify God." That is the reason we are here on earth—to glorify God. If we profane His name, we are moving against the very reason God put us here. If something does the very opposite of what it was designed to do, where does such a thing end up? It ends up in the garbage heap. That garbage heap is called Gehenna, or Hell. Though the chief end of man is to glorify God and to enjoy Him forever, those who do not fulfill their purpose in this world will end up separated from Him forever. God gave this commandment to protect us from this tragic fate.

GOD'S NAME IS HOLY

In many churches the Lord's Prayer is recited as part of the worship service. Perhaps you pray it at home. Let's think for a minute about the first petition: "Our Father, which art in heaven, hallowed be Thy name." In all that we do—at home, at work, at the beach or a dinner party—we should acknowledge that God's name is holy. This should be our prayer every day and every hour that we might spend our lives to the glory of God, and that we might speak of Him with reverence as the altogether glorious person He is.

The Jews of the Old Testament most definitely understood the need to show reverence for God by honoring His name. The scribes who copied Scriptures by hand had many, many complex rules that enabled them to copy the writings very carefully and accurately. One of them was that whenever they came to any of the secondary names for God—such as El, El Shaddai, Elohim, or many others—they stopped and put down their pens. They took up new pens and carefully wrote that name. But a very different rule applied when they came to the principal name that God had used to reveal Himself, the name "Jehovah," for which they used the four letters YHWH. Before they wrote this highest and best name, they rose from their seats and went into their personal quarters. They took off their robes, bathed themselves, clothed themselves with new, clean garments, and returned to their work. There they knelt down, confessed their sins, took a new pen, dunked it once into the ink well, and wrote those four letters, YHWH—for Yahweh.

Compare this with the way we sling God's name like mud against the walls of our conversation, and you will realize the depravity of man's heart. Yes, I know the excuses people bring:

"Well, I didn't mean anything by it."

"Oh, you know, it's . . . it's just a bad habit."

"I didn't even realize I was doing it."

That is the problem.

When God said in Exodus 20:7, "You shall not take the name of the Lord your God in vain," He was saying, "Do not use My name for emptiness—for no purpose, for no reason, as if My name has no significance."

That is exactly what some people do. That in itself is a tragedy. However, the greater tragedy is that of all the sins we commit, we enter into this sin without temptation or provocation. If we are having a difficult time, we should call upon the almighty God,

Maker of the universe, Creator of life, to help us. There is no good reason for misusing His name.

A minister had a tire that was almost flat. He pulled into a country gas station and asked the attendant if he could fix it. As the man filled the tire and checked the water and a few other things, he kept repeating, "G—— D—— this tire," and "G—— D—— this" part of the car, and "G—— D——" that. Finally, the minister could stand it no longer. He spoke up: "Sir, I do not want God to damn my car, and I'll thank you to stop saying that."

The attendant gave a predictable response: "Oh, I didn't mean anything by it. I . . . ah . . . it's just a habit. I didn't mean to offend you. I didn't even realize I was doing it."

Again and again people claim: "I didn't know. It just slipped out." That is not really the truth, is it? If you profane God's name, you know that you do it. Remember when Richard Nixon, president of the United States, had his Oval Office tapes transcribed and printed in the newspaper? As you may recall, every other sentence contained profanity or blasphemy of some sort. I was shocked when I read it. I was horrified that the president of the United States was such a blasphemous man. Not only horrified—it told me something about Mr. Nixon. Billy Graham had known Nixon for more than thirty years, and Dr. Graham told me personally that during those years he had never once heard a profane or blasphemous word come out of Nixon's mouth. The tapes revealed to me that Nixon knew quite well what he was doing, when he was doing it, and who was around when he did it.

There is another response people give when they realize they have used God's name in vain in front of another person, as is illustrated by a story I heard about Woodrow Wilson's father, a Presbyterian clergyman. One time, a man took the name of God in vain—then saw Reverend Wilson standing nearby. Embarrassed, he said, "Oh, excuse me, Reverend Wilson, I didn't realize you were there."

The reply was, "Sir, your apology is not owed to me."

Isn't it amazing what practical atheism is revealed by a person who is concerned that he may offend a clergyman, but the same man is not concerned at all about offending the omnipotent God who has commanded him not to take His name in vain?

A COMMANDMENT WITH A CONSEQUENCE

The truth is that blasphemy has become a habit of our society. It is all around us. Does this mean it doesn't matter? It matters so much to God that He warns us of serious consequences for committing the sin of blasphemy.

Even if everyone in the world lifted his eyes to heaven and cursed God in unison, it would still matter. It would still be an affront to almighty God. There was a time in history when the whole world did this very thing, and God judged them with the flood that swept away the human race. We forget this sometimes. We have the erroneous idea that God takes a poll to see if the majority of people have crossed the line. If they have, perhaps He will change His standard. But that is not the way it happened in Noah's day. The whole world was "only evil continually" (Genesis 6:5), and God destroyed every last person on this earth, except for Noah and his family of eight.

Have we forgotten that out of every grain of sand on every beach in this world, God can create another person if He wishes to do so? God could create a billion times as many people as there are here . . . just like that!

God is serious about His name. In the Bible a name represents a person, just as it does in this case. You are concerned for the reputation of your good name. We have laws against people who would slander your name because, when they do, they slander your person. For those who hold God in contempt and drag His name down in the mud, there is a penalty. God says, "The Lord will not hold him guiltless who takes His name in vain" (Exodus 20:7). This is no idle threat. It is a statement of a fact. One theologian said that it is the calmly awful fact of eternity. It is no different from the fact of gravity. According to the law of gravity, if you step off the roof of a thirty-story building, you will die. That is not a threat, because a threat has the potential to happen or not to happen. It is a fact. And if you take the name of God in vain, it is a fact that God will not hold you guiltless. But just what does that mean—not to hold us guiltless? It means that we shall not go unpunished.

You see, when God is diminished, when God is held up in mockery and irreverence, when God's honor is trampled, God is not affected at all. No. God Himself does not die, as Nietzsche predicted. God remains very much alive, as He was in every other century before this one and will be in every century that is yet to come. But when the existence of the Life-Giver is held in contempt, then the lives of men are also held in contempt. If God is degraded, we become as cheap as grains of sand. We come to the death of man. That is a pretty serious consequence, don't you agree?

We saw in the twentieth century the deaths of more than 40 million babies taken from the womb, many millions of people tortured and killed by Hitler, some 135 million killed by atheistic Communists. But it was man they killed, not God—as Nietzsche predicted. Because God loves us, He told us to reverence His name, knowing that we—not He—would experience the consequence if we failed to do so.

But man, in his vanity, tries to pull God down. You know, I have discovered that, generally speaking, it is the little man who has a vile mouth. It is the little man who attempts to put God down in order to build himself up. It's a vain attempt that results only in making that person look contemptuous in the sight of decent men and certainly in the sight of our holy God.

I remember the story of a man almost twenty-five years ago, a member of another church. In that church, he was the head of a society that supposedly honored the name of Jesus. Yet he told about his descent into all kinds of depravity, including a time when he blasphemed the name of Jesus. He told how he expected a lightning bolt to strike him, but nothing happened. Again he misused the name of Jesus. And again and again until, finally, it became a habit. Sadly, I watched that man's life disintegrate, and I thought about God's promise in Exodus: "The Lord will not hold him guiltless who takes His name in vain" (Exodus 20:7). Remember that you do not reap in the same season that which you sow. I am absolutely confident that many people are experiencing this and yet they have no idea why.

How many times have you and I heard people ask, "Why? Why did this happen to me?" "Why did my child die?" "Why did my wife leave me?" "Why did my husband abandon me?" "Why did I lose my job?" "Why do I have this disease or that disease (or a hundred others that are rotting the body)?" "Why are all these terrible things happening?" "What did I do?" And the lament is coming out, in some cases, between lips stained with blasphemy, and they don't even know why. To such people, I would say, "O foolish men, are you blind, are you deaf, have you no mind? Have you not heard what the Lord has said, that He 'will not hold him guiltless who takes His name in vain'?" Perhaps you are even now experiencing the inevitable—what God has promised. The Lord will not hold him guiltless. The Lord will not let him go unpunished who takes His name in vain.

PROCLAIMING GOD'S NAME

As God's children, we need to be different from the majority who profane His name. We need to proclaim His name and lift it up to His glory. We need to speak out as God's people.

You may have heard of Sir Christopher Wren, perhaps the greatest architect who ever lived. He designed many marvelous buildings, including St. Paul's Cathedral in London. He was a devout Christian who sought to bring honor and glory to God. That is why Sir Christopher Wren designed the cathedral and also superintended the building of it. He ordered a sign to be placed in several locations on that construction site that said this: "Due to the heinous custom of laborers to take the name of God in vain, each person is hereby placed on notice that it shall be sufficient cause for immediate dismissal if the name of God is heard taken in vain in this place." Now there is a man I can look up to—a man who put himself on the line to honor God.

BREAKING THE HABIT

If such signs were put up today, would any building ever be completed? I truly doubt it because of the vileness and the foulness of the mouths of many people, even some "religious" people who go to church and pray, "Hallowed be Thy name."

Some people may say, "Well, yes, but I've been doing it for years. It's a habit. I don't think I could break it." My friend, let me tell you this. It is, without any doubt, the easiest habit to break. There is nothing to it.

Let me give you an example that is very close to home for me. As a young man in my late teens and early twenties, I occasionally used profanity. I am sorry to say that I even used the name of God in vain. Then I learned of the immense love of Jesus Christ. I learned that on the Cross, He was in agony for me. I learned that what He was enduring, He was enduring for my sake and in my place and in my stead. The wrath of God for my sins was falling upon His head as my substitute. When the impact of this dawned on me, I fell to my knees. With many tears, I invited Jesus into my heart to be the Lord and Savior of my life. That was in 1955. To the best of my remembrance, I have not one time in the nearly fifty years since taken the name of Jesus Christ in vain.

Now, you may think, *Oh, he just wants a pat on the back for his faithfulness.* Not at all! If that is what you are thinking, you do not understand what we have been talking about. I say that because it is now the easiest conceivable thing in the world for me not to profane the name of Jesus. That day forty-seven years ago, I fell in love with Jesus, and I have never had the slightest temptation to take His name in vain. I have not resisted any temptation. It is not there, because I would never do anything to offend Him.

Let me ask you a question: Do you love your mother? Would you use her name as a curse word? How do you resist those temptations that come every day to curse in the name of your mother? My guess is that the thought has never entered your mind because you love her. Do you see that people take the name of God in vain because they don't love Him?

Someone once said to me of a woman he knew, "Oh, yes, I know she takes God's name in vain all the time, but she really has a heart of gold." Can this be true? Jesus said, "Out of the abundance of the heart the mouth speaks" (Matthew 12:34). That woman's heart is in rebellion against God Almighty, her Creator. That is why she takes the name of God in vain, because she has no love for Him. Her heart is not a heart of gold. It is a heart of sin, and no matter what we think, it will be revealed as a rebellious heart on that great day when God reveals all hearts.

My opinion is that how a person uses or misuses God's name reveals whether a person is converted, whether a person is a Christian, whether a person has been saved and has been born of the Spirit of God and transformed. Not everyone who refuses to curse is a Christian, but every obedient Christian does not take God's name in vain.

ARE YOU HIS?

Are you a Christian? Has the truth been revealed? Has your mouth betrayed you? As onlookers said to Peter during the trial of Jesus, "Thou art a Galilaean, and thy speech agreeth thereto" (Mark 14:70 KJV). And the betrayal here is of something worse than being from rural Galilee. It is a betrayal of the fact that Christ has never changed our hearts. We have never become new creatures. The love of Jesus Christ does not fill us and cause us to want to glorify Him, to want us to hallow His name. No unrepentant blasphemer shall enter heaven (Revelation 21:27). The Bible declares it.

Are you really a Christian? Is that your curse word? If so, it shows that you hold Christ in contempt of depravity. Yes, my friend, this is a very serious commandment, and it reveals how many people in our society are utterly alienated from God.

My friend, I know this is a heavy lesson, but let me leave you with a word of hope. Just as God forgave Saul of Tarsus (1 Timothy 1:13), God forgave me forty-seven years ago for my disregard for His name. He will forgive you and anyone else who sincerely repents of the sin of blasphemy. He will help you change your habits and give you a heart overflowing with words of praise. Listen to these words from Psalm 66:

> Come and hear, all you who fear God,
> And I will declare what He has done for my soul.
> I cried to Him with my mouth,
> And He was extolled with my tongue.
> If I regard iniquity in my heart,

The Lord will not hear.
But certainly God has heard me;
He has attended to the voice of my prayer.
Blessed be God,
Who has not turned away my prayer,
Nor His mercy from me! (vv. 16-20)

Lift words of praise and glory to your Maker now! He is listening and will bend down to hear you, to forgive you, and to place His words of praise and glory in your mouth.

Heavenly Father, help me to fall in love with You today. Help me to look unto Christ and see the agony He endured, the infinite wrath that was poured out upon Him for our sake. O Jesus, I have not realized until now that You endured all of that because of me. The wrath of God was poured out upon You because of my vileness, because of my profanity, because of my blasphemy.

O God, help me to look at Your beloved Son, whom You have loved everlastingly, Your only Begotten, and realize that when my sin, my profanity, was placed upon Him, even He did not go unpunished. In His name I pray. Amen.

CHAPTER FIVE

The Gift of Rest

In those days I saw people in Judah treading winepresses on the Sabbath, and bringing in sheaves, and loading donkeys with wine, grapes, figs, and all kinds of burdens, which they brought into Jerusalem on the Sabbath day. And I warned them about the day on which they were selling provisions. Men of Tyre dwelt there also, who brought in fish and all kinds of goods, and sold them on the Sabbath to the children of Judah and in Jerusalem.

Then I contended with the nobles of Judah, and said to them, "What evil thing is this that you do, by which you profane the Sabbath day? Did not your fathers do thus, and did not our God bring all this disaster on us and on this city? Yet you bring added wrath on Israel by profaning the Sabbath."

So it was, at the gates of Jerusalem, as it began to be dark before the Sabbath, that I commanded the gates to be shut, and charged that they must not be opened till after the Sabbath. Then I posted some of my servants at the gates, so that no burdens would be brought in on the Sabbath day.

—NEHEMIAH 13:15-19

Remember the Sabbath day, to keep it holy.

—EXODUS 20:8

IT IS UNDOUBTEDLY one of the great paradoxes of life in the twenty-first century: Our homes are full of labor-saving devices that are supposed to make our lives easier than ever, and yet most people have never worked harder—or perhaps it is more accurate to say we have never been busier. At no other time in history have human beings been in such a hurry to get wherever it is they are going. (I am convinced that many people rushing through life at 100 miles an hour have no idea at all where they are headed.)

With our pocket calendars and computerized handheld organizers, we have never been so determined to cram every minute full of frenzied activity. Oddly enough, we have never had less time to do the things that are really important. Every year, new studies reveal that Western people spend less and less time with their spouses, their children, their neighbors, and their God.

How did we ever come to this unfortunate, frantic state?

One way we got here, surely, is by always striving for more, more, more in terms of material things. Nicer homes, more land, better cars, more fashionable furniture. We are also striving to fill the empty spaces of our lives with noise and tumult to keep us from noticing the emptiness inside. We want more friends, more social contacts, and more fun.

The problem is that when we get these things, every one of them demands more time and attention. Our homes need cleaning and repair. Our cars need washing and waxing and maintenance. Our furniture needs dusting. Our friends want time and attention. Our social clubs demand participation in activities. Our fun requires money, and to get money, we have to work harder and longer. So we are getting more and doing more, and life zips by as we are devoured by tiny, bite-size ticks of the clock.

Many pastors and spiritual counselors encounter this complaint on a regular basis: "I am burned out, physically fatigued, emotionally drained, and spiritually empty. What should I do?"

"You need some rest," the counselor replies. "Do you ever take a break?"

Rest? They can't believe what they just heard. Suggesting they give up something, anything, from their rat race of activities brings a look to their faces as if you had just abused them. "Rest? With all I have to do? You must be joking." Perhaps they are looking for a special secret that will make all of the unenjoyable and demanding things of life go away, so they can then fill their days with leisure-time activities.

But the "secret" is already out—if we will do what God has already commanded.

GOD COMMANDS US TO REST

God so loved the human race that He gave us the Sabbath—a day of rest each week. Do you realize how remarkable that is? Why, God is the ultimate authority. He is the Boss, so to speak. Have you ever had a job where your boss told you to take it easy because you were working too hard? I didn't think so. Instead, bosses would be more likely to say things like, "Get off your duff and get back to work!" or "Can you reschedule your vacation? I really need you here!" But not God. He says, "Rest."

In fact, the very word "Sabbath" is derived from the Hebrew *Shabbath* which means, very simply, "rest." A few years ago, *Omni* magazine printed a story on research into the workings of the human body that discovered something believers have known for centuries. The human body is designed so that it works best if one day out of every seven is given to rest. God knew what He was doing when He told us to honor the Sabbath day. That's no surprise, since He invented the human body and knows what it takes to maintain it.

The amazing thing is that some people just don't understand. I think about Pastor Ron Mehl, who writes about the day he woke up in a hospital bed after serious cardiac surgery. The first thing he saw swimming in front of his eyes, all out of focus, was a human countenance. When he finally was able to focus, he discovered that the face belonged to a pastor friend, who asked him, "Well, is that good enough for you?"

Pastor Mehl couldn't believe what he was hearing. He thought, *What kind of a question is that to ask a man who has just had a severe heart attack?* But it was about to get worse.

"Are you proud of yourself now? You really think you are something, don't you?" the man asked.

His friend had tried to talk to him like this before, but Pastor Mehl usually just turned and ran to another appointment or something else he had to do. But with all of the tubes sticking out of his body, he couldn't do anything but lie there and take it, and his friend wasn't nearly through.

"You think you are so smart. You think everyone is impressed because you, the pastor, work seven days a week. You have to be there every day, or it won't get done. Now look at you. Look what you have done. You have been disobedient to God for all of these years, and now here you are. Is this good enough for you, or do you have to kill yourself altogether?"[1]

Ron Mehl decided, as he lay there in that hospital bed, that things would be different from then on. I hope it doesn't take a heart attack, or some other serious physical or emotional health crisis, to get you to understand your need for rest.

Before the state, before the Church, before even the family, the first institution God gave to mankind was the Sabbath. Having created the heavens and the earth and all things therein, He rested on the seventh day and blessed the seventh day and hallowed it, and He commands us to keep it as such because He loves us. And if we love Him, we will love His Sabbath.

WHICH DAY SHOULD WE OBSERVE?

Some people get distracted on this matter of keeping the Sabbath holy. In a moment we will come back to God's reasons, beyond personal health needs, for telling us to keep the Sabbath. But since there is confusion on the matter of which day we should observe, it is well worth our examining this issue briefly.

Some claim that we are not observing the true Sabbath unless we are observing it on Saturday. They ask, "How did the Sabbath change from Saturday to Sunday?" Some will tell you that the Emperor Constantine changed the Sabbath about A.D. 325 simply because he was the Caesar of Rome and had the power to do so. But what Constantine really did was to make Sunday a legal holiday so Christians wouldn't have to worship in the catacombs before dawn on Sunday morning and then go to work.

In fact, the day of the Sabbath was changed by Christ and His apostles. You see, Saturday was originally designated as the Sabbath as a commemoration of the Creation—as Genesis tells us, the Lord created the heavens and the earth in six days and rested on the seventh. So the Jews celebrated the Creation of the physical heavens and earth. We Christians, on the other hand, celebrate the resurrection of Christ and the creation of the new heavens and the new earth—the everlasting kingdom that was brought into being by His resurrection and victory over death.

Here are just a few of the reasons why Christians observe Sunday, the first day of the week, as the Sabbath:

Christ rose from the dead on the first day of the week. After His resurrection, He appeared to Mary Magdalene, Mary the mother of James, and Salome on the first day of the week. He appeared to the disciples, all except Thomas, on the first day of the week.

A week later, again on Sunday, He appeared to them again, and that time Thomas was there.

According to Acts 2, the Holy Spirit was poured out upon the apostles on the Day of Pentecost, which was the first day of the week.

It was on the first day of the week that the disciples came together to celebrate the Lord's Supper (Acts 20:7). The apostle Paul told Christians to give their tithes and offerings on the first day of the week (1 Corinthians 16); the apostle John described the first day of the week as "the Lord's Day" (Revelation 1:10).

This transition from observing the Sabbath on Saturday to celebrating it on Sunday happened long before Constantine came to power. For example, in A.D. 120, no more than twenty-five years after the apostle John died, Barnabas, one of the earliest of the apostolic fathers, wrote, "That they keep the eighth day [first day of the week] with joyfulness, the day in which Jesus rose from the dead."[2] According to the Eastern way of reckoning time, Sunday would be the first day of the week, as well as the eighth day, when the days of the week begin all over again.

Just thirty years later, around A.D. 150, Justin Martyr, one of the earliest martyrs of the Church, said, "Sunday is the day on which we all hold our communion assembly because Jesus Christ, our Savior, on the same day arose from the dead."

And then, in A.D. 194, one of the great Church fathers, Clement of Alexandria, saluted a fellow Christian by saying,

"He, in fulfillment of the precept according to the Gospel, keeps the Lord's Day"—which, as we've already discussed, is Sunday, the first day of the week.

As a final witness, we can turn to Tertullian, another of the early Church fathers. He said, in A.D. 200: "We solemnize the day after Saturday in contradiction to those who call that day their Sabbath."

So did Constantine the Great change the Sabbath? Not at all. He simply recognized the day Christians had been celebrating for three hundred years. The first day of the week, the Lord's Day, is the Christian Sabbath—our day of rest, joy, and gladness.

WHY DON'T WE KEEP THE SABBATH?

I believe it is very important for Christians to understand why the Sabbath eventually moved from Saturday to Sunday. Unfortunately, some people get so caught up in arguments about when the Sabbath should be observed that they forget to consider the *why* of the day. They don't think about why God gave us the Sabbath or why it is so urgently needed.

The question we really need to ask here is: Why do people go on dishonoring God, pushing Him out of their lives? Why are they unwilling to give Him so much as one hour a week for worship? Some people don't honor the Sabbath because they say Sunday morning is the only time they have to spend with their families. There are two reasons why that's not a valid excuse:

First, there is no better place than church to spend time with your family.

Second, if Sunday morning is the only time you have been able to set aside for your family, you need to reorder your priorities. Your family should be more important to you than that.

Now, I know what many people say. Some insist they can get closer to God out in His creation—hunting, fishing, or picnicking by a rolling stream. That might be a great way to spend the rest of the Sabbath. But God wants you to be in church with your fellow Christians at least part of the time that day. Hebrews 10:25 urges us, as Christians, not to quit meeting together on Sunday, but to encourage one another to take part in the weekly assembly. Sunday morning worship is important to God, and because of this, it should be important to every Christian.

Still others will tell you they don't need to be in the worship service on Sunday because the Church is full of hypocrites. Perhaps that is true, but as the old saying puts it, "The Church is a hospital for sinners, not a museum for saints."

I could go on for pages listing the excuses I've heard from people who just can't find the time to honor the Sabbath, but in the end it comes down to this: If the Sabbath is important enough to God that He would issue a commandment about it, we must understand that it's important to us, too. It is past the time that Christians should take back the Sabbath, find rest, and honor God.

Time is a very precious commodity. You can't take it back and start over again. Once it's gone, it's gone forever. We're all given fifty-two weeks a year to use, and every week contains seven days with twenty-four hours each. What are you doing with the time God has given you? Are you spending it the way He wants you to? Are you using part of it to rest in God, as He commands you?

An old French proverb says, "He was born a man. He died a

grocer." Now, believe me, I have nothing at all against grocers—since many years ago I became happily accustomed to enjoying food! But whether we're talking about a grocer, a car salesman, an insurance man, or a man or woman who practices any other profession, how tragic it is that anything done to earn money should be the sum total of a person's existence. The person who may be summed up with the words, "He was a grocer," certainly did not use his time the way God would have wanted him to. What a lessening of the value of a man made in the image of the eternal God.

We can turn our situation around if we reinvest time with its proper value. That is, we can treat the Lord's Day as a chance to stop, look away from all of the things of this earth, gain spiritual perspective from focusing on God, and realize that His purposes are more important than the lesser things with which we fill our days. When we do this, we bring sanity and godliness back to the management of our lives.

I heard a story about a man who had just taken over the presidency of a large corporation. An aide told the president that there was a very important meeting called for the next day at ten o'clock. He said, "I'm sorry. I won't be able to be there."

The aide said, "But, sir, this is regarding a very important matter. It's a crisis that must be dealt with."

The new president just shook his head and said, "I'm sorry, but I have a previous appointment. I can't make it."

His aide said, "Sir, I'd really like to know what appointment means so much to you that you can't break it for something as important as this."

The president smiled and explained, "I have an appointment

with the Lord God Almighty tomorrow at ten-thirty, in His house, at His table, and I will be there."

This man's name was James Garfield. He went on to become president of the United States, and he definitely had his priorities straight.

Here's what another very busy man—J. C. Penney—had to say about honoring the Sabbath: "If a man's business requires so much of his time that he cannot attend the Sunday morning and evening services, and Wednesday night prayer meeting [of his church], then that man has more business than God intended him to have." Penney insisted on remembering the Sabbath day and keeping it holy, and he still built one of the world's largest department store chains.

KEEP THE SABBATH AND KEEP THE NATION

Have you ever heard the old saying, "As goes the Sabbath, so goes the nation"? It's true. When the Sabbath becomes profaned and desecrated, a nation sinks deeper and deeper into the mire of sin, and that has a profound negative impact upon any country. If we are looking for another practical reason to keep the Sabbath holy, here, surely, is an urgent one.

Christians need to understand that keeping the Sabbath really does create a more moral climate in our culture. It promotes an awareness that God and His ways and His laws are important to all of us. Without public morality, our secular laws have less meaning; the result is that lawlessness rises, and our nation sinks into crime, fear, disorder, and injustice.

From the witness of the early Church, from the witness of our disarrayed lives, from the witness of our society as it teeters on the brink of moral collapse, we can see that the need to keep the Sabbath is truly urgent.

Did you know that your grandfather probably referred to Sunday as the Holy Sabbath? Your father probably called it Sunday. We call it the weekend. We are demeaning the Sabbath, and we are doing so at our peril.

SHOW YOUR FAITH TO THE WORLD

Another thing happens when you honor the Sabbath by getting up and going to church on Sunday morning. That is, you show the world that you believe in Jesus Christ. If you say you belong to Jesus, but sleep in every Sunday morning, your neighbors are going to think that your faith doesn't mean very much to you. And you know what? They'll be right!

On the other hand, when you get up, get dressed, and go to Sunday morning worship, you are joining millions of people all over the world in testifying to the fact that Jesus Christ rose from the dead. Nothing else could have caused His early followers to abandon their seventh-day worship. Jesus Christ's resurrection from the dead changed the world in many dramatic ways, and one of these was the institution of a new day to honor and keep holy. It is a good witness to Christ to honor the Sabbath and keep it holy.

And while we're talking about the importance of being a good witness, here's something else to consider. From my study of the Scriptures, I believe that we Christians are to abstain from secular work on the Sabbath, with three exceptions: (1) works of mercy, such as those performed by doctors, nurses, paramedics, and firefighters; (2) works of necessity, such as eating; and (3) works related directly to God and His kingdom. But I believe it's not enough for us to abstain from working on the Sabbath. We must also do what we can to avoid causing others to work on this holy day. Think about it for a moment: Do you go out to eat on the Lord's Day? If you do, you are obviously making people work to feed you.

I remember a Sunday evening a long time ago when my wife and I went out for dinner and were the only people in a little counter-style restaurant. I struck up a conversation with the cook (who was also the waiter, cashier, and everything else). When I found out he was a Christian, I asked him where he went to church.

He shook his head. "I don't go to church," he replied.

Well, of course, I told him that he ought to be in church on Sunday, that it was really important. And I asked him why he did not go.

Suddenly, he whirled on me, waving his spatula in my direction. "Why don't I go to church?" he asked. "I'll tell you. I don't go to church because of people like you who come in here and make me work all day long to feed you. That's why."

I was speechless. I had never thought that some of the things I did on Sunday, such as eating out, might be keeping others from spending time with the Lord. Certainly, this man had his own choices to make in the matter. Blaming anyone else for our failures to obey God is always a smoke screen. But I truly learned something for myself that day. Mainly, that there is much more to keeping the Sabbath than just going to church on Sunday morning.

EXPERIENCE THE JOY

Before we move on, I want to give you my final, and best, reason for obeying this fourth commandment: Great joy comes from taking the time to rest in the Lord—from spending more time in the Scriptures, more time in prayer, more time in fellowship with other Christians.

Anyone who ignores the Sabbath is really missing out. What is more, he or she will wear out before his or her time. God is your loving heavenly Father, saying, "Rest, My child. Rest." You will live longer. You will be happier, you will be healthier, and your relationship with God will be vastly improved.

Jesus invited, "Come to Me, all you who labor and are heavy laden, and I will give you rest" (Matthew 11:28).

Heavenly Father, we pray that Your Spirit will speak to our hearts. We thank You, O God, that we are not saved by keeping your commandments because we know that we have broken every one of them in word or thought or deed, and so we are guilty. As You have said, "There is none righteous, no, not one" (Rom. 3:10). We are guilty, and we have been condemned already. Thus, we thank You that You have sent Your Son as a far greater Gift than the Sabbath. We thank You that He endured for us the agonies we deserve, in order that we might receive what we do not deserve, the free gift of eternal life, for simply trusting in and receiving Jesus Christ, in whose blessed name we make our prayer. Amen.

CHAPTER SIX

Learning to Honor Your Parents

Moses said, "Honor your father and your mother"; and, "He who curses father or mother, let him be put to death." But you say, "If a man says to his father or mother, 'Whatever profit you might have received from me is Corban'—" (that is, a gift to God), then you no longer let him do anything for his father or his mother, making the word of God of no effect through your tradition which you have handed down. And many such things you do.

—MARK 7:10-13

Honor your father and your mother, that your days may be long upon the land which the LORD *your God is giving you.*

—EXODUS 20:12

ONCE THERE WAS an older man whose eyes blinked more than they should have and whose hands trembled uncontrollably. Because he had no place to live, he moved in with his son's family. The son's wife wasn't exactly thrilled with the new arrangement, and she especially hated it at the dinner table, where the constant clinking of his silverware and sloshing of his drinks were more than she could bear. Finally, in her anger and exasperation, she insisted that he eat his meals alone in the corner, separated from the rest of the family.

He began to eat alone, looking wistfully at the family sitting at the table. But then one day his hands were shaking so much that he knocked his bowl on the floor, spilling his meal onto the brand-new carpet.

"That just does it!" the daughter-in-law screamed. "If you're going to eat like a pig, we'll feed you like a pig!" She made a wooden trough, put it on the floor, and told him that he would have to eat out of the trough. So he did.

Then one afternoon, a few days later, the woman's little boy came in the house excited about something he had made. "Look,

Mommy!" he shouted. "I made a trough to feed you and Daddy out of when I get big."

She didn't say a word. She just began to cry, and from that day forward, the older man ate his meals at the table with the rest of the family. It didn't matter anymore how much noise he made with his silverware or how much of his drink he sloshed on the table. In fact, the daughter-in-law did everything she could to make up for the horrible way she had treated him.

If the story I've just told sounds vaguely familiar, that's because it's been around since the early 1800s. It is a fairy tale from the Brothers Grimm, but like many fairy tales, there's a great deal to think about in this children's story. People today don't make their elderly parents eat out of a trough on the floor (at least, I hope they don't), but many take their mothers and fathers to what amount to warehouses for elderly people and abandon them. These people have forgotten the fifth commandment, which says, "Honor your father and your mother, that your days may be long upon the land which the Lord your God is giving you" (Exodus 20:12).

In the sixth chapter of Ephesians, Paul writes that this is the first commandment with a promise. There are really two promises connected to this commandment, because in Deuteronomy 5:16, when the admonition to honor our parents is repeated, God says, ". . . that your days may be long, and that it may be well with you."

We have in this commandment a promise of both prosperity and longevity. This does not mean that everyone who honors his father and mother is going to live long and be rich. But as a general principle, this is true.

WHEN YOUR PARENTS ARE DISHONORABLE

People have said to me, "Well, Dr. Kennedy, I'm sure this commandment can't apply to me. My parents were horrible to me when I was growing up. Surely, God can't expect me to honor them."

Oh, yes, He does!

For an example of men who honored a parent who was behaving dishonorably, take a look at Genesis 8–9. Almost as soon as the waters from the Great Flood had abated, Noah planted a vineyard.

Now the plot thickens. . . .

As soon as the grapes were ready, Noah made wine and then got so drunk that he passed out naked in his tent. He was in that condition when one of his three sons, Ham, saw him. And what did Ham do? He immediately went out and told his two brothers about the shameful thing their father had done. But those brothers, Shem and Japheth, honored Noah more than Ham did. They took a blanket, went into their father's tent, and covered him up. The Bible goes on to tell us that Ham was cursed, as were his descendants, for failing to honor his father, even though Noah's behavior was clearly dishonorable.

In the same way, we are required to show honor to our parents, no matter what their behavior might be. I know that it is hard to honor a parent who has never caused you anything but grief. What form that honor takes is up to you. One woman grew up in a home where her mother had a violent temper. For no reason at all, her mother sometimes slapped, punched, or verbally abused her. But today, as an adult living several hundred miles away from her family, she honors her mother by sending her flowers on her birthday and Mother's Day. These may seem small gestures, but I am certain they are pleasing to God.

I am just as certain that the children of celebrities who have written tell-all books about their parents are displeasing to Him.

PARENTS, DON'T SHIRK YOUR RESPONSIBILITY

Does this mean that when it comes to this commandment, parents don't have any obligation toward their children? Of course not! Your children will not honor you unless you teach them to.

I have visited in the homes of many families where the children seemed intent on destroying everything in the house, including the peace of mind and happiness of their parents. Meanwhile, the parents did nothing about it. Children who are not disciplined and taught to honor their parents while they are young will not honor them when they are older.

The commandment to honor parents means *children* should respect their parents and hold them in high esteem. Both their tone of voice and attitude of heart should communicate respect and honor for their parents. Children who are thus instructed will live a long, full life. But the Bible also promises a very serious judgment against the child who disobeys and refuses to honor his parents: "The eye that mocks his father, and scorns obedience to his mother, the ravens of the valley will pick it out, and the young eagles will eat it" (Proverbs 30:17).

Parents who want their children to have a long life and not God's judgment must demand respect and honor from them. The happy consequence of that for their children will be not problems and turmoil but an enjoyable, prosperous future.

We must teach our children to obey the Bible's admonition: "Children, obey your parents in the Lord, for this is right" (Ephesians 6:1).

In recent years, some doctors, psychologists, and educators have said, in direct opposition to the Bible, "Children, do whatever you want to do. The important thing is to let it all hang out. Self-expression is the most important thing."

It doesn't take a Ph.D. to see what this kind of thinking has brought us. So many times "experts" have challenged the Bible on an important issue like this one. When that happens, all we have to do is wait a few years and discover that their worldly wisdom has been a recipe for catastrophe. When will we learn to take God's Word for what it is—the wisdom of the almighty and omniscient God—and follow it?

OUR NATION IS AT STAKE

Certainly, the health of the individual family hinges on obedience to this fifth commandment, but much more is at risk as well. I believe that as goes the family, so goes the nation. If children do not respect their parents, they are not likely to respect any kind of authority, and thus, a nation where children do not respect their parents is bound to fall.

If Junior doesn't learn respect at home, he is not going to respect or honor his teachers in school. When he gets a little older, he will not respect the law. A nation with too many Juniors cannot succeed. Every time I read my morning newspaper, it is evident to me that we are heading rapidly in that direction.

You see, the fifth commandment about honoring the authority of parents also applies to teachers and police and any other authority that might be placed over you, including your boss.

Having been the senior pastor of Coral Ridge Presbyterian Church for forty-two years, I have seen a number of people fired from their jobs for various reasons. But as I think back over them, I see that poor job performance was very rarely the reason. In most cases, the problem was one of attitude, a rebellion against authority. Why? Because they never learned respect for authority at home. "Why has my life been so miserable?" they ask. "Why do I have so much trouble in so many different areas?" Because they never learned to honor their father and their mother.

They have no respect for any type of authority, they are not thankful for anything they have been given, and ultimately, they will bring their entire nation to ruin. There are many historical examples.

Persia became the first of the great world empires because Persians trained their children to be obedient. But eventually things changed, because the Persians had grown wealthy, which brought about a relaxed discipline, which led, in turn, to sin, and then to the downfall of the nation.

Then came the Greeks, whose discipline was legendary. The Spartans, for example, were so strict that when a young man entered the army, he was given a shield and told: "Come back with it or on it, but don't drop it and flee, and don't surrender. Either fight 'til you die or 'til you gain the victory." Thus it was that 300 Spartan soldiers turned back about 10,000 of their enemy at Thermopylae. But the Greeks became self-satisfied; they failed to teach their children the importance of honoring their parents, and their empire faded into history.

The Roman Empire was the next to arise, due principally to the *patria potestas*—the absolute total rule of the father over the son—which was in force as long as father and son should live. The son could own nothing, could do nothing, could go nowhere without the permission of his father. That iron discipline enabled the Romans to conquer the entire known world. But then, like the Persians and Greeks before them, they forgot all about the importance of honor and respect for parents and produced such monsters as Nero, who showed how much he honored his mother by committing her to a terrible death. Rome was swallowed up by God's judgment in history.

Time and again, the deterioration of children's respect for their parents has affected the history of the world. We must teach our children to honor their fathers and mothers—not in the extreme ways of Sparta or Rome, but according to the Bible.

IT'S OKAY TO BE A MAMA'S BOY

In today's world, some children don't show honor to their parents because they are afraid their friends will call them a "mama's boy" or a "daddy's girl." But you know, there is nothing at all wrong with being a mama's boy.

I think of a young man who wanted desperately to join the

navy and see the world. He dreamed of being captain of a ship someday. What a thrill that would be!

His mother, however, was not thrilled by the idea of her son, who was just sixteen, going off to sea. She walked with him down to the port, and just as he was getting ready to leave, she said to him, "Son, I just have no peace about your going off to sea. I have prayed a great deal about this, and I really wish you wouldn't go."

What did this young man do? He said to one of the other sailors there, "I cannot sail off and break my mother's heart," and he went home with her.

He never became the captain of a ship, but he did go on to command an entire navy, as president of the United States. The young man was George Washington, who had been taught the Ten Commandments as a child and knew the importance of honoring his father and mother.

WARNING TO PARENTS

Before moving on, I want to give this word of warning to parents. Although discipline is important, it must never be administered in anger.

If you are angry because of something your child has done, take a few moments to cool down before you impose discipline. Otherwise, the punishment may be harsher than the disobedience deserves, and you may be guilty of provoking your child to wrath, which the Bible condemns in Ephesians 6:4.

It always fell to me to spank our daughter—which I think happened only about half a dozen times—and whenever I did, I would take her into her room and tell her: "You know, honey, Daddy loves you. But God has placed you under my authority, and I'm to rear you to become an obedient, honorable child. Therefore, when you disobey, I have to spank you. I don't like to do it, but I'm doing it for your own good." (I must admit, though, she never really got that message very well.)

I believe that when your children's behavior forces you to punish them, you must do it in love and let them know that you are disciplining them not because you are angry with them, but because you want them to be the best persons they can possibly be—the person God intended each of them to be.

A WORD OF WARNING FOR CHILDREN

There is something quite unique about the fifth commandment. Do you know what it is? It is the only commandment you do not have to keep all of your life. In fact, you can't keep it after your parents have died because it's too late. If your parents are still living, the time to honor them is now. If you have not been showing them the respect and honor they deserve—the respect and honor God wants you to show them—I urge you to change your behavior immediately, before it is too late.

I can attest to you that even though my parents left this world years ago, there are many things I wish I had another opportunity to do better. Again, if your parents are living, I hope you will show them the honor and respect demanded by this fifth of the Ten Commandments.

HEALING IN YOUR FATHER'S ARMS

Even if it is too late for you to honor your parents, and even if you have spent your life in an attitude of rebellion, God wants to set you free from your shame and guilt.

To help you understand how much He loves you, please consider with me the biblical story of David and his son Absalom.

King David loved Absalom with an enormous love. But Absalom was a rebel who usurped his father's kingdom and precipitated a war. As David's soldiers were getting ready to go out to war against Absalom and his men, David had one word to his generals: "Deal gently for my sake with the young man" (2 Samuel 18:5).

Now, as Absalom was riding furiously through the forest on a mule, his long hair became tangled in the branches of an oak tree and the mule rode out from under him (v. 9) and left him dangling by his hair. That is how Joab, one of David's generals, found him. Even though he had heard David's admonition to "deal gently," he took a spear and plunged it into Absalom's heart—and then another one and another one—leaving Absalom's dead body hanging from the tree.

In Jerusalem, when David received the news that his rebellious son was dead, he was crushed. Absalom's death meant that David's throne had been restored. But at that moment, he gladly would have traded his kingdom for his son's life. In sorrow, he made his way to a room above the gate of the city, and there he cried, "O my son Absalom—my son, my son Absalom—if only I had died in your place! O Absalom my son, my son!" (2 Samuel 18:33).

No matter how David's heart was aching, he could not die for his rebel son. But a greater King, and a greater Father, has also had His heart broken by the rebellion of His children. That Father is God. The rebels are you and me. When we rebelled against Him, He did not merely wish that He could have died for us; He came in the person of His own Son and did, indeed, suffer and die in our behalf.

It was not because of any goodness in us that God was willing to die for us, but because of His grace. He died in our place that we might be forgiven, that our rebellious hearts might be traded for hearts of love and faithfulness—and that we might be adopted back into the family of our Father and our King.

Have you experienced the new life that Christ can bring, the realization that all of your sins are washed away? Today, it is possible—because of the atoning sacrifice of Christ—for you to stand before God as one who has never rebelled against Him, as one who has always shown honor and respect to your earthly parents. If you have not yet accepted Christ's sacrifice in your behalf for the sin of dishonoring your father and mother, I urge you to do it.

Heavenly Father, we pray that You will cleanse us and forgive us of all of our sins, which can be done only because of the suffering and agony that Your Son endured in our place and in our stead. We invite Him into our hearts. We trust in Him as our Savior. By His grace we repent of all of our sins and ask that henceforth we might stand clothed in perfect righteousness—the righteousness of Your Son, in whose name we pray. Amen.

CHAPTER SEVEN

Thou Shalt Do No Murder

Cain talked with Abel his brother; and it came to pass, when they were in the field, that Cain rose up against Abel his brother and killed him.

Then the LORD *said to Cain, "Where is Abel your brother?"*

He said, "I do not know. Am I my brother's keeper?"

And He said, "What have you done? The voice of your brother's blood cries out to Me from the ground. So now you are cursed from the earth, which has opened its mouth to receive your brother's blood from your hand."

—GENESIS 4:8-11

You shall not murder.

—EXODUS 20:13

Whoever sheds man's blood,
By man his blood shall be shed;
For in the image of God
He made man.

—GENESIS 9:6

TRACING GENEALOGIES IS a very popular hobby these days. Some people spend hours tracking down sources on the Internet or poring over records in the archives of libraries as they search for their family history. Sometimes they run into surprises. Perhaps they discover a prestigious relative perched on a branch of the family tree—someone famous whose life pursuits and accomplishments left a positive legacy for the generations to follow. On the other hand, they may stumble upon an infamous character—a relative who did not live such a good life. How would you feel if you discovered your ancestors were thieves—or worse? I guess if you are going to delve into your family history, you should brace yourself to face whatever you find!

I can tell you one thing for sure. No matter who you are, there is at least one relative in your family lineage who was a murderer. In fact, you are related to the very first murderer. We all are. His name was Cain, and he was also the very first person to be born on planet Earth. Now, Cain had a brother named Abel. He was the second person to be born on this planet and the very first murder victim.

Just one generation into human history, man's murderous tendencies emerged. It didn't take long for us to show our true colors, did it? The seeds of sin were planted by Cain and Abel's parents, and already the roots were going deep. This murderous tendency escalated at an alarming rate until the earth was filled with violence. God was grieved and angered by man's disregard for life. His just outrage was so intense that He decided to cleanse the earth and start over again.

A FRESH START

God did this by preserving the family of one righteous man named Noah. When the flood waters receded, God issued three commandments. One of them, recorded in Genesis 9:6, states, "Whoever sheds man's blood, by man his blood shall be shed; for in the image of God He made man."

Through these words, God reveals His deep concern about the sanctity of the life He created. Human life is so important to Him that He issued a universal law. It was not given solely to the chosen Jews or to any other group. It was given to the entire new world and has never been countermanded. Yet when we come to the book of Exodus and the giving of the Ten Commandments, we read in the beginning of the second table of the law—which contains laws governing our relationships to one another—these four simple words: "You shall not murder."

At first glance, it would seem that there is a contradiction in Scripture. How skeptics love to point to these two seemingly opposing scriptural statements in Genesis and Exodus in an effort to cast doubts upon the credibility of God's Word! But stick with me and you will see by the end of this chapter that if we really understand what these verses mean, it is clear that God did not contradict Himself.

MAN'S INTERPRETATIONS OF GOD'S LAWS

We have to be careful when we quote Scripture. We need to be sure that we are not taking God's words out of the context in which they were given. Otherwise we might present an erroneous picture to the world of God's character. Let me give you two examples:

A few decades ago, crowds of college students regularly marched in the streets of America's cities and passionately protested the war in Vietnam. Placards were raised high into the air printed with the words: THOU SHALT NOT KILL. These young people truly believed in their hearts that the sixth commandment prohibited the war in Vietnam, and if it prohibited that war, it must prohibit *all* war.

After four years on death row, Timothy McVeigh was executed as dawn began to break early one Monday morning. He had confessed, without remorse, to what was then the most violent terrorist act in United States history—the Oklahoma City bombing that took the lives of more than 150 people, including helpless babies and innocent children. No one could argue that McVeigh was not a cold-blooded murderer. Yet on the night before his execution, a crowd gathered to protest outside the prison where he was being held. What was the basis for their objection to Timothy McVeigh's execution? It was, most certainly, the sixth commandment, "Thou shalt not kill" (Exodus 20:13 KJV).

There are other examples I could cite, but the point I am making is that if you simply look at the words, "Thou shalt not kill," it would seem that God is saying that it is never justifiable to take another person's life. That would mean that we should not go to war as a nation to defend our beliefs, our rights, or the human rights of others who are being mistreated. It would mean that executing murderers who are guilty beyond a shadow of a doubt of capital offenses would be prohibited. Is this really what God commands?

Sometimes people cite this commandment when they are sitting down at a meal of carrots, celery, and lettuce. They believe that "thou shalt not kill" means we should not end animal life. Still others take it to another extreme, influenced by certain Eastern religions that maintain you shouldn't kill any living creature—even a mosquito or a bug. If a mosquito should land on your arm, you can flick it off, but you should not kill it!

WHAT DOES GOD MEAN?

Many people try to make this commandment say what they want it to say. But what matters is what God says. Like a putty nose, you can twist Scripture and pull it and shape it any way you want it to look. You can make the Bible say anything you want it to say—as long as you ignore the laws that govern the interpretation of Scripture.

There are three basic laws:

1. We examine the sentence or block of text to see if we understand what it is saying, in and of itself, without any outside explanation.
2. We examine the passage in context to ensure that we do not pull a text out of context and make that a pretext for whatever we would like to have it say.
3. We examine the passage in light of the whole of Scripture—that is, in the broadest context of the whole Bible.

When we have done these things, we can understand what the text means, and then we can be sure we have not made it say anything we want it to say. It will speak to us of what God intended for us to hear.

APPLYING THE LAWS OF INTERPRETATION

Now we return to the commandment: "Thou shalt not kill." Using these three principles, let's look at this text to see if its meaning becomes clear.

In this case, we are dealing with a text in translation from the Hebrew Old Testament. So we have to go back to the original text to see what is said in the original language. Interestingly, in Hebrew there are about nine different words that can be translated as "kill." Moses passed over eight other words that mean things like "to kill," "to slaughter," "to sacrifice," or "to slay." These usually refer to animal sacrifices. He bypassed all of them and chose the word *ratsach*, which means "murder." It always means "murder." Therefore, the text should be translated, as it is in almost every modern English translation of the Bible: "You shall not murder."

If you have any doubt about this translation, appeal to the second and third laws of interpretation. Examine the immediate context of this commandment, and consider the passage in the light of the whole of Scripture.

To do this, let's look at a command recorded in Genesis. This is the command I mentioned earlier that was given by God just after the Great Flood. He said, "Whoever sheds man's blood, by man his blood shall be shed; for in the image of God He made man" (Genesis 9:6).

A very important point to note here is that man, unlike a chicken or a pig, is the only creature made in the image of God. Therefore, human life is sacred to Him. Referring to the birds of the air, Jesus said, "Are you not of more value than they?" (Matthew 6:26). God values the life of man so much that He says a murderer must pay with his own blood for the life he takes from another. You see, murder is such a grievous sin to God because it is an attack upon those who are made in His image. It is an indirect attack on God Himself.

GOD MAKES HIMSELF PERFECTLY CLEAR

Since the punishment must fit the crime, we have one consequence for stepping on the grass or jaywalking, another for stealing a package of gum from the drugstore, another for stealing a car, and another one for manslaughter, which is the act of accidentally killing somebody. But God calls for the highest penalty to be required of the one who commits the greatest crime. The bottom line is that if you willfully take the life of another person, God requires that you pay for it by losing your life.

The passage from Genesis 9:6 is not the only one in Scripture that says this. In Exodus 21 you will find six different specific circumstances where God commands the taking of life. If "thou shalt not kill" in Exodus 20 means that we are, under no circumstances, to take the life of anyone else, we obviously have a contradiction between Exodus 20 and 21, which are side by side in the Bible. God has suddenly become schizophrenic, He has forgotten what He said in the last chapter, or the Bible is irreconcilable even to itself.

But let's review a few of these six places in Exodus 21 where we are commanded to take life:

- Verse 12 records, "He who strikes a man so that he dies shall surely be put to death." A different word is used here, *mooth,* than the Hebrew *ratsach,* which means "to murder."
- In verse 15, we are told that "he who strikes his father or his mother shall surely be put to death."

- Verse 16 states, "He who kidnaps a man and sells him, or if he is found in his hand, shall surely be put to death."
- And in verse 17 we read, "He who curses his father or his mother shall surely be put to death."

In Exodus 21 alone, God identifies six very specific and grave circumstances that are so offensive to Him that they require the death penalty. It is obvious that the text is clarifying that killing is never acceptable to Him. Even so, God strictly forbids murder. If we commit murder, willfully and intentionally, we forfeit our lives.

GOD'S COMMANDMENT FOR TODAY

What about some of the more modern interpretations of this commandment we hear espoused today? Does "thou shalt not kill" mean we are not to carry out capital punishment, as some insist? We have seen that the very first person born was a murderer. But have we not become more civilized since Cain killed Abel? Have we not become more caring, loving people—so much so that we wouldn't even think about murdering anyone? I don't think that is the case. In the decade of the 1990s, we Americans murdered about 14 million of our own—babies who were killed by their mothers before they took a single breath of air. I hardly think we have become so civilized that we no longer need God's commandment.

Even if you apply the third law of interpretation and look at the full context of Scripture, you will see that in the New Testament the Ten Commandments are repeated a number of times. Each time they are repeated, it says, "Thou shalt do no murder." One who commits that crime—*phoneuo* in Greek—is a murderer and nothing else.

We have a great need for clarity about that today. Does it mean that if a person has been convicted of a capital crime and has been sentenced to death, we can wave a placard saying, THOU SHALT NOT KILL, and stay the execution? Not at all. In this case, the criminal justice system is in accord with God's universal commandment that was given to the human race after the Great Flood. If a person has willfully slain another person who is made in God's image, he owes the debt of his life in return.

And in the case of abortion? Is that a violation of the law? I remember one time, years ago, I spoke on the subject of abortion, and a couple approached me and said, "We assume, therefore, that you do not believe in capital punishment if you are pro-life."

I said, "On the contrary, I do believe in capital punishment."

They replied with an accusation: "You are not consistent."

I said, "Oh, really. Well, let me ask you: Do you believe in abortion?"

The man said, "Absolutely. It's a woman's right. A woman has a right over her body."

In a certain sense this is true, of course. In another, it is not. Technically speaking, it's not her body she is killing. It is another of God's living creatures, another person who has entirely different DNA. There is a fifty-fifty chance that the baby she carries is not even the same sex as she is.

Taking the discussion a step further, I asked the couple, "Do you believe in capital punishment?"

They said, "Absolutely not."

I said, "It seems to me that the difference between us is very simple. I believe in sparing the life of the innocent and taking the life of the guilty, whereas you believe in killing the innocent and sparing the guilty. But the Bible says that God hates 'hands that shed innocent blood' (Proverbs 6:17) and 'Woe unto him that calls evil good and good evil' " (Isaiah 5:20).

And that is exactly what we have been doing in this country. We have been killing the innocent and sparing the guilty, and I believe that God is displeased with this transgression of His specific command.

KILLING TAKES MANY FORMS

What about the matter of suicide? I received a letter from a woman who said that until she heard me speak on the subject of suicide, she never realized that it was a sin. Scripture records only five cases of suicide, and all of them are reported with condemnation.[1] You see, suicide is a form of murder. When someone takes his life, he is still taking the life of a person made in the image of God. It is taking the precious gift of life that God gave to him, and he is flinging it back into God's face as if to say, "I don't want it." That is the murder of the self, which is actually what suicide means.

You may argue, "What if a person is in constant pain? Doesn't he have the right to take his life? Surely, in such a case a person has the right to find peace." I do not believe that person will find the peace he craves by killing himself. Those who die without the covering of Christ's gracious sacrifice face greater future torment than the aches and pains of this world.

I speak with some empathy for the person suffering intense and chronic pain. There has hardly been a day in the last twenty-five years that I have not experienced pain of some degree that ranges between serious and excruciating. When I get tired and discouraged, as I sometimes do, should I kill myself? No. I am thankful to God for each day of life and for the work to do for Him.

Another debate surrounds the killing that occurs in the event of war. No one would argue about the fact that war is a horrible thing. Nor would anyone dispute that many wars have been fought without righteous justification. But the Christian Church has maintained that there is something called a "just war." This springs from the principle of self-defense. If an evil intruder enters your home with the intent of killing you or your family, civil laws are in place to protect you from such wanton criminality and murder. One law permits you to kill the intruder if your life or the lives of your family are at stake.

Similarly, in a just war, when your country is attacked by an aggressor and you are called upon to defend it, killing may be necessary. Defensive killing is forgiven and accepted as a necessary evil, but an offensive war is condemned. The point is, tragically, that lives are always lost in a war, and the aggressor country technically commits murder. Christians serving in the armed forces must give careful consideration to the battles they are being called upon to fight. Is it a defensive war or an offensive battle to help the country aggrandize itself against some other nation? It makes a difference in God's eyes.

A POSITIVE PERSPECTIVE

Now that we have examined the sixth commandment from different angles, we see that it is not quite as simple as it first appears. A modern translation says, "You shall not murder," which lends some clarity to the issue. But in spite of the gravity of the sin of murder, there is a positive side to this commandment, and there is good news, even for those who break it.

In Old Testament times, a murderer could flee to one of the cities of refuge and there find sanctuary until his case was decided. In the New Testament, we are told that in Christ we find divine forgiveness, though we may still have to suffer the temporal consequences of our actions.

If you are guilty of killing someone—even your own child—there is mercy with the Lord. It is offered conditionally, however. You must recognize the horror of your sin and confess it with a truly repentant heart. When you do, the blood of Jesus washes you clean and frees you from condemnation.

THE LESSON OF THE GOOD SAMARITAN

Let me remind you of a scriptural example that illustrates this. Do you remember the story of the Good Samaritan? He came along and found a man who had been brutally beaten and left to die along the side of the road. The priest and the Levite—those who would be expected to show compassion—passed by the man and kept right on walking. But the Good Samaritan—the outcast—stopped and cared gently for the man, cleansing and bandaging his wounds. He took the beaten man to an inn, gave the innkeeper money for his care, and promised to provide more, if necessary, upon his return.

Do you know that the Good Samaritan was obeying the sixth commandment to the full degree? You see, God not only does not want us to take the life of another, but also wants us to provide for and enhance life whenever we can. How can we do this? In many ways, such as feeding and helping people in dire need. When we do this, we are not taking their lives, and we are providing what they need to stay alive.

Ultimately, we all bear this responsibility. So let us think for a moment about practical ways you might fulfill this positive side of the sixth commandment:

- Can you give some of your time to be a big brother or sister to a child who is alone—perhaps a child from a broken family who needs a Christian friend and role model?
- Is there a lonely, elderly man or woman in your family or neighborhood who would be blessed to have you visit on a regular basis? Can you give of your time to enhance the dwindling days of that person's life?
- How about an example that is even closer to home? How can you build a better life for your children, who are growing up faster than you can imagine? Could you cut back on your work load or personal commit-

ments to spend more quality time with them? You will be investing time in those precious children's lives and futures. It is time you cannot recover, once it has slipped away.

- What about that person at work you just can't relate to? Maybe you clash, and there is hostility or tension between you. Rather than harboring ill feelings and avoiding that person in the lunchroom, would you be willing to demonstrate the meekness of Christ by going out of your way to begin a friendly conversation? You may have a chance to witness and be used by God to bring that person to Christ.

SPIRITUAL NURTURING

Another way to obey the sixth commandment in a positive way is to make sure we do not neglect to care for people who are suffering spiritually. We would never expect in our day and age for a priest or Levite to come along and pass by someone who is beaten, as in the story of the Good Samaritan. However, are we not just like the priest and Levite when, day after day, we pass by people who have been beaten and bloodied by Satan and sin?

When people's lives are in ruins and they are in jeopardy of coming unredeemed before the judgment seat of God, are we not "killing" them by not sharing the healing power of the Gospel? We who have the Spirit of Christ within us and know that only He can bring hope, forgiveness, and a new life—how can we just pass by those who are perishing in sin, right before our very eyes?

Have I hit a nerve? Suddenly, are you thinking, *Dr. Kennedy has crossed over the line from preaching to meddling?* So be it! My goal in writing this book is not to be popular, but to motivate my readers to apply the valuable lessons we can learn from this study of the Ten Commandments.

I challenge you now to examine your heart and ask yourself if you truly believe God. Do you really love the human beings He created in His image? Will you pass by and let someone die without hope, without Christ, without God? Let us not only avoid the sin of physical murder and killing, but let us also endeavor to fulfill the other side of the sixth commandment. Let us seek to enhance the physical lives of others and to be channels to impart spiritual life whenever God provides opportunities for us to be used as His witnesses.

LET LOVE RULE

It has been rightly said that the greatest commentary on the sixth commandment is found in the thirteenth chapter of 1 Corinthians. You may recall this marvelous letter written by the apostle Paul. In it, he defines love. He describes the opposite of murder as being our responsibility to love our neighbors, to love strangers, to love our enemies, and to minister to their needs. As sinful people, we cannot fulfill this in and of ourselves. But God grants us the grace to love. It's not easy, but it is a blessed thing, and God will see that those who are guilty will be punished and those who have been obedient will be blessed.

That is why Christ came into the world. That is why His Father poured out His wrath for sin upon His beloved Son and, thereby, offers freely to pardon and grant eternal life to all of those who choose to trust in Him. There—upon that Cross—a murder took place. It was the most heinous, vicious murder ever committed in past, present, or future history. At Calvary, mankind's sin resulted in the murder of God's own Son. He submitted willingly so that we—the very people responsible for His suffering and death—might, in turn, find life and joy forevermore. Have you found it?

Heavenly Father, how gracious and glorious You are. How wondrous are Your grace and mercy. I pray that I might never stubbornly reject Your love, but always come to Jesus Christ for cleansing and forgiveness. Wash me, Father, and make my soul whiter than snow! Then use me as a vessel to enhance the lives of others and to draw them to You, lest they come before Your judgment with guilt upon their heads. And now be with me and bless me each day of my life. Help me to be a life giver and not a life taker. In Jesus' name. Amen.

CHAPTER EIGHT

The Sexual Revolution

[Jesus told them,] "You have heard that it was said to those of old, 'You shall not commit adultery.' But I say to you that whoever looks at a woman to lust for her has already committed adultery with her in his heart."

—MATTHEW 5:27-28

You shall not commit adultery.

—EXODUS 20:14

UNLESS YOU HAVE been residing on the moon for the past four decades, you know that America and other countries of the world have been through a revolution. I'm referring to the so-called "sexual revolution."

I think the word "revolution" is the right one to describe what has happened in terms of sexuality. The great revolutions of history have occurred at times when people revolted against governments or ideologies they could no longer endure. Our own American Revolution comes to mind, when our ancestors united to revolt against King George III of England. The French Revolution is another example where the masses rebelled against the authority of a leader, King Louis XVI. The modern sexual revolution is, indeed, a revolt against something.

But against whom is the sexual revolution directed? The answer, very simply, is that this revolt is an uprising against God. It is a rebellion against His sovereign authority and right to be Ruler. It is a rejection of His law.

On a TV talk show, several famous people were having a

discussion about this topic. One woman posed the question, "Is there any room in our culture today for morals?"

Someone answered quickly, "No."

End of discussion! Nobody challenged this blunt statement—this dismissal of a moral basis on which to found society and individual behavior. Nobody said, "How can you say there is no room for morality?" or "On what authority do you say that?" No one objected or reacted with remorse. This is the way it goes in our culture in the twenty-first century. The authority of God and the law of God are summarily rejected without question or discussion.

You see, popular opinion maintains that we have been emancipated from ancient and repressive ideas. As Randy Alcorn, author of *Restoring Sexual Sanity*, put it sardonically:

> The moral "ice age" is over. Exit the dogmatic dinosaurs of sexual repression. Enter the sensuous sirens of sexual expression. We live in the age of sexual enlightenment, presumably but a few years from sexual utopia.[1]

If you ask any "enlightened" American what he thinks about traditional morality, you will likely get this sort of response: "Well, it went out with washboards and penny candy. Nobody believes that stuff anymore, except folks who still use push lawn mowers and manual typewriters."

IN THE NAME OF PROGRESS

We certainly don't want to be like those "unenlightened" folks, do we? We are all for "progress"! We want to fit in. We want to be modern and advanced. We want to be up on the newest trends. Freud—and many psychologists who followed him—said that we should explore and express the fullness of our sexual nature. Hang-ups, old taboos, and superstitions must go! That is the way many Christians are tempted to think, despite what they may say about their commitment to God and their personal relationship with Him through faith in Jesus Christ.

Someone has written:

> Sexual anarchy is here. It has assumed extreme forms and spread throughout a large part of the population, side by side with an increase of sexual perversions; a shameless sexual promiscuity has also greatly increased. They seduce members of the same family. Relations between father and daughter, son and mother are not unknown. In fact, contemporary authors rejoice in relationships with two sisters or a mother and a daughter. Adultery, rape, and prostitution have greatly increased. Homosexual love has entered the mores of the population, and contemporary authors seem sadistically to enjoy the enumeration of a variety of . . . sexual perversions.

I suppose you are thinking this was written by someone describing our modern-day society and culture. Not exactly. This quote is not from the pen of a contemporary author. The writer lived 4,500 years ago, around 2500 B.C., in ancient Egypt.

THE ROOTS OF THE REVOLUTION

The sexual revolution is old news. It is not modern. No, it's as old as sin. In fact, the revolt began with the lie of the devil: "You will not surely die . . . [but your mind will be expanded] knowing good and evil" (Genesis 3:4-5). The irony of that lie, when Adam and Eve bought it, is that they did die—first spiritually and later physically. The other irony is that today, for all our talk of sexual revolution and freedom, we still don't know the difference between good and evil. We can't see that "free sex" without commitment is not good, or that abandoning spouse and family to a life of struggle and misery in order to find your "personal happiness" is a terrible and destructive mistake.

This first lie of Satan was like a seedling the devil planted, and we can see how it grew like weeds in the mind of man. Once the enemy convinced us that wrong was right, the revolution was on. But Satan did not stop with the first lie. He has continued to bombard the world with lies that we have bought into—lies that keep us in a state of moral degradation because they facilitate our rationalization that wrong is right. For example, you don't have to look far these days to find this situation:

John's marriage was stale. The "passion" was gone. So when Sue began flirting with him at the office, he was on shaky ground. What could be the harm in flirting back, if it made him feel alive? Or, so he thought. A little flirting led these two down a path to a predictable destination. They had an affair. Eventually John's wife found out. Hurt and outraged, she kicked John out and filed for divorce. Now he lives in a dumpy apartment, because he can't afford to pay for two nice homes. Most of his paycheck goes for alimony and child support. The worst part of it is that John can no longer see his kids every day. He misses them terribly and would do anything to get them back. He should have thought about that before he convinced himself that nothing was wrong with a little office flirtation.

Do you see how Satan so easily convinces us that we are able to decide for ourselves, apart from God and His law, what is right and wrong? But we can't because there is only one standard of righteousness—God's standard. We have believed a lie, and so we act in rebellion against the eternal truth.

Perhaps we need to stop and examine some of the lies we have come to accept as truth. As we do, I want you to keep in mind that society's perception of Satan is also based on a lie. We don't take him seriously because we picture him the way he is depicted in cartoons, movies, and books—the little red devil with horns and a monstrous face. We see him as an evil demon who causes furniture to fly around the room and people to go out the windows and all kinds of supernatural things to happen. This is nonsense!

Satan is described in Scripture as a liar—indeed, the father of lies (John 8:44). Satan deceived mankind from the very beginning, and he still employs lies as one of his primary weapons against us—lies that poison our minds, our hearts, and our very souls—lies that we buy into, with deadly consequences. We just examined one of them. But there are more.

LIES OF THE SEXUAL REVOLUTION

One of the lies people buy into today is that the sexual permissiveness of our times is part of "the new morality."

It is not moral, and it is certainly not new. Sexual permissiveness, and the pain and confusion it brings, is as old as sexuality itself. But millions of Americans have bought the lie, and it has helped us rationalize wrong behavior and take us down to the moral level that prevails today.

Another lie is expressed in a statement like this: "Sex is a private matter between two consenting adults. After all, what I do is nobody else's business."

That has a nice ring to it, doesn't it? It seems logical. As long as it's nobody else's business, then nobody else gets hurt. That is where the line of reasoning supposedly leads.

Nothing could be farther from the truth. The fact is that sexual choices are not a private matter at all. Everyone in America is paying for the private affairs of others—literally thousands of dollars each year pay for the sexual sins of the "enlightened ones." Sexual permissiveness has brought about the births of literally millions of illegitimate children. All of these children have mothers, and many of them are unwed mothers. Today, unwed mothers are the new poor— mothers without husbands or fathers who live on welfare and cost the rest of us millions and millions of dollars every year. Children who grow up without fathers too often end up in inner-city gangs. We all pay for this—not just with money, but with fear over the crimes these angry, confused children are prone to commit. We all pay for the so-called private choices made by individuals.

We need to recognize this for the tremendous social problem it is. Today, in Los Angeles, there are more gang members than there are police officers. Many, if not most, of the young men and women in these gangs come from single-parent and broken homes—products of the great sexual revolution. According to police officials in L.A., these gang members are full of anger at a world that has ignored them and left them on their own. They are better armed than the police, so law enforcement officers are outnumbered and outgunned. That is what they face every day.

Again—who is paying for this mounting war, this direct result of sexual revolution against God's laws? You and I are.

No, we cannot say truthfully that sexual choices are entirely an individual and private matter.

A third lie that many have bought into is that we must set ourselves free from the repression of traditional Christian morality if we want to be free to experience real mental health. This attitude is an outgrowth of Sigmund Freud's psychological theories from the turn of the last century.

Freud believed that religion was some kind of neurosis, and that we should not repress our feelings. According to Freud, we need to stop repressing our feelings and desires and simply "let it all hang out." I remember the 1960s as the "let it all hang out" decade. It was a time when people were urged to act on all their desires. If you conformed to any religious or social standards, so the countercultural gurus said, you would end up in a mental institution. If you lived by "old-fashioned," traditional, biblical values . . . if you believed in being sexually chaste until marriage . . . if you believed in fidelity in marriage . . . you were looked down upon. You had to be insane!

Well, how true is it—this idea that sexual chastity, self-control, and lifelong commitment breed mental illness? Dr. Francis Braceland is a former president of the American Psychiatric Association, which is not exactly an evangelical Christian organization. Dr. Braceland has also been the editor of *The American Journal of Psychiatry*. Certainly, his professional credentials qualify him as an expert on mental illness. Braceland spoke at a Methodist conference on medicine and theology, indicating, according to a *Christianity Today* article, that premarital sex relations growing out of the so-called new morality have significantly increased the number of young people in mental hospitals. Braceland told the Methodist gathering that "a more lenient attitude on campus about premarital sex experience has imposed stresses on some college women severe enough to cause emotional breakdown."[2]

Hold on here! What was that? A psychiatrist who is not speaking as a Christian maintains that sexual permissiveness has caused mental illness not to decrease, but to significantly increase.

Furthermore, sexual problems and confusions and relational complications that result from permissiveness are known to be a primary factor that leads to suicide among high school and college students. We need to examine this tragedy in light of all this talk about a wonderful sexual revolution and freedom. Bear this in mind when some handsome guy tells you how wonderful a sexual encounter is going to be, and when he tells you, "If you love me, you'll be intimate with me." The truth is, if he loves you, he will not ask you to break God's law and throw yourself open to mental, emotional, and spiritual turmoil!

A fourth lie has been lobbed into our midst by the enemy. This time the argument goes: No smart-thinking, responsible person would buy an automobile without test-driving it, so why should we enter into a marriage without testing sexual compatibility?

Again, much energy has gone into convincing people that this line of reasoning is just good common sense. But sociologists have recently completed some studies that reveal an interesting and indisputable fact: There is a much higher incidence of divorce among people who live together before marriage than among people who do not. Furthermore, among those who lived together before marriage, there is a much higher incidence of infidelity during marriage.[3] There is a much lower incidence of infidelity in marriage among couples who respect and obey God's commandments regarding sexual morality.

Yet another lie: Young people, especially, are being told—often in public school curriculums paid for by the tax dollars of good, moral Christians—that to be emotionally healthy and well-balanced, they must develop their sexual identity. Subtly and not so subtly, our young people are being encouraged to embrace immorality and flout God's law.

One psychologist and her colleagues decided to test the theory that sexual experimentation "develops" personality and personal identity. Under scientific conditions, they administered the well-known Minnesota Multiphasic Personality Inventory (MMPI). This standardized test is used in mental health centers across

America. Psychologists gave the test to a group of people who were highly "sexually active."

Can you guess what they discovered? Do you suppose these sexual adventurers were more emotionally balanced, more psychologically healthy, or more mature than their sexually inactive counterparts? Not by far. In fact, about half of these people demonstrated abnormal depression, introversion, nervous activity, and even some delusional thinking. The other half of the test group scored extremely low on the truth-telling scale. As a group, they were most certainly not well-adjusted, healthy, mature human beings.

WHY WE BELIEVE THE LIES

When you consider the sad realities of the sexual revolution, it is puzzling that people believe these lies about sexual freedom. Obviously, the lives and experiences of millions of people bear out the fact that if we break God's law, we suffer, and we cause others to suffer. In the face of so much suffering and confusion, why are so many so willing to demand their sexual freedom?

One reason people fall into sin and error—first in thinking, then in actions—is that words are very powerful. The media and leaders of so-called "social liberation" groups twist and manipulate words, persuading many to believe that immorality is moral. We see, for instance, how a young woman is manipulated to think of her "right of choice," and that it alone is supreme, and so she is convinced that choosing abortion is not murder. After all, the rhetoric goes, what she's carrying in her womb is not really a person, but just the "product of conception." As a result, she may have an abortion, believing she will experience no physical, mental, emotional, or spiritual consequences. She is sold on the idea that it will be no different from going through a procedure to remove a wart or a mole. Because the vocabulary is changed and words are twisted, the thinking is twisted. Sadly, the results of abortion are as tragic and real for the mother as for the child.

Here is another illustration of my point about the warping of our vocabulary. On a talk radio show one day, the subject was adultery. The host of the show said, "We'd like for any of you out there who have committed adultery to call in. Let's discuss that experience on our show today." The host and his guest speaker waited . . . and waited. The phone lines were silent, as if they were dead. Finally, the host rephrased his invitation. This time he said, "If any of you out there have had an affair, call in and let's discuss it." Immediately, the lines lit up!

You see, the word "adultery" convicts people. No one wants to admit committing adultery. But the concept of having an affair has become acceptable to people. When people called in, they insisted that what they'd done was "no big deal"; they felt "good" about themselves, as if they'd done something "daring" or "heroic." Call it what you will, adultery is adultery, but by changing the term, it has come to mean something acceptable.

A more important reason why we buy into the lies of the sexual revolution is that we are ignorant of God's truth. In most homes, God's Word is grossly neglected; adults ignore it entirely.

Children grow up without any knowledge at all of who God is or what His laws command us to do.

A young man said to me recently, "Dr. Kennedy, I know that having sex with a married person is wrong. But what about two unmarried people having sex—is that all right?"

"The Bible says that fornication is a sin," I replied.

The young man, who was in his twenties, looked very puzzled. "What's fornication?"

"Fornication refers to sex between two unmarried people," I said patiently, but firmly. "Clearly, God wants us to know that it's wrong for two unmarried people to have sex."

He thanked me for answering his question, but I was amazed at his ignorance of the Word of God.

Are you clear about God's Word and what it says on matters of sexuality? The Bible warns that neither adulterers nor fornicators nor homosexuals have any inheritance in the kingdom of God (1 Corinthians 6:9). I am not the one who says this. God says it in His Word.

The Bible is very clear about another, more major issue. Everyone who disobeys God's law hates Him, and those who hate God love death (Proverbs 8:36). People demonstrate their hatred of God and His laws time and again by their rebellion and rejection of His rule over them. God is the living God. He is the God of life. He is the Giver of life. He is the One who promises, to those who obey His Gospel, life everlasting and life abundant. Whenever you reject His commandments, you reject Him, and you inevitably bring death upon yourself.

A third reason people buy into the lies of the sexual revolution is that they want to be "emancipated" and "free." They are taught to assert their right to self-expression. They are encouraged to believe sexual liberty will make them better, healthier people.

However, we are in the midst of a sexual epidemic. Right now, rampant in this country are twenty-nine different sexually transmitted diseases. Millions of people are suffering with new strains of diseases that will not yield to even the strongest drugs. Some people have several of these diseases, with symptoms so terrible they cannot be described here.

The tragic fact is that by buying into contemporary lies about sexual freedom, by flaunting God's laws, we are reaping the consequences. One study maintains that the average life span of a married heterosexual American male is seventy-six years, while the average life span of a homosexual American male is just forty-one years.[4] It would appear that a man forfeits about half of his life by buying the lie that homosexuality is a normal, healthy alternative to God's established sexual standard.

Nevertheless some voices in our culture insist that traditional morality has kept America from blossoming into the wonderful nation that it could be. You have only to open a history book, and you will discover that no matter how far you study—to the old kingdom of the Egyptians, the Assyrians, the Babylonians, the Medes and the Persians, the Greeks and the Romans—there is a historical pattern that repeats itself again and again. First, there is an era of discipline when people control their urges. Society blossoms; kingdoms flourish. Gradually, the attainment of wealth and success causes a loosening of the bands of discipline and self-control. In this second phase of the pattern, society after society plummets to destruction. Throughout world history, this pattern has repeated itself more than twenty-six times.

Where do we stand as a nation? I fear we are on the downhill slide.

THE TRUTH THAT CAN SET US FREE

This is a very serious matter, and one that grieves God, who loves us and does not want us to be destroyed. Many people in our nation have traded the truth of God and the law of God for a lie and for rebellion. But there is hope.

One of the tragic things about all sin is that it is addictive. Whether it's sex, drugs, alcohol, overeating, or gambling—it doesn't matter what sin you fall prey to, it is addictive. And the more you do it, the stronger the addiction becomes. Are you in bondage to sexual sin right now?

The good news is that the shackles that chain you have already been broken at Calvary. There on the Cross, Christ died to free you from captivity to every sin, including the strong bonds of sexual sin. He can set you free. You can go to that fountain and be washed and cleansed. You can be clothed in the perfect righteousness of His robes of purity and become whiter than snow. You can become truly free by repenting of your sin. This is the only hope you have in this sinful world.

I invite you, in His name, to come to the Cross to find forgiveness, to find a new life, to find purity, which I know that some readers desire.

Are you involved in a sexual relationship right now that is in direct violation of God's seventh commandment? Do not listen to the lie that can keep you from repenting and turning to God. The whispered lie that says, "You are the worst of sinners. Do you really think God is going to forgive you?" Consider the way our Lord Jesus dealt with those who wanted to stone to death a woman caught in the very act of adultery:

> The scribes and Pharisees brought to Him a woman caught in adultery. And when they had set her in the midst, they said to Him, "Teacher, this woman was caught in adultery, in the very act. Now Moses, in the law, commanded us that such should be stoned. But what do You say?"
>
> This they said, testing Him, that they might have something of which to accuse Him. But Jesus stooped down and wrote on the ground with His finger, as though He did not hear. So when they continued asking Him, He raised Himself up and said to them, "He who is without sin among you, let him throw a stone at her first." And again He stooped down and wrote on the ground. Then those who heard it, being convicted by their conscience, went out one by one, beginning with the oldest even to the last. And Jesus was left alone, and the woman standing in the midst.
>
> When Jesus had raised Himself up and saw no one but the woman, He said to her, "Woman, where are those accusers of yours? Has no one condemned you?" She said, "No one, Lord."
>
> And Jesus said to her, "Neither do I condemn you; go and sin no more" (John 8:3-11).

My friend, Jesus has set you free to enjoy a life of fullness and joy. You can put the past behind you—no matter what sexual transgressions you may have committed. Take the Savior's words to heart: "Go and sin no more." Go and enjoy an intimate relationship within the boundaries God has established for your good. Renounce the lies of Satan, and embrace God's truth. It is the only way to be set free.

Heavenly Father, deliver me from the lies of Satan. May my eyes be opened to see the deceitfulness of the devil, and seeing it, and seeing how I have been ensnared, may I come to hate my sin, to see myself as impure, to cry out, "Unclean, O God, I am unclean. Wash me or I die." I pray that I might be cleansed by the blood of Christ even as now I pray, O Lord Jesus. It was for me that You have suffered and died. It was my sin that put You upon that Cross.

Father, I repent of those sins. I am sorry for them. Deliver me from them and make me free. Help me to live a life of sexual purity, and grant me the intimacy of a marriage that You can bless, because it is founded in faithful obedience to Your commandments. I pray in Your most holy name. Amen.

CHAPTER NINE

If You Can't Do the Time, Don't Do the Crime

"Has this house, which is called by My name, become a den of thieves in your eyes? Behold, I, even I, have seen it," says the L*ORD.*

"But go now to My place which was in Shiloh, where I set My name at the first, and see what I did to it because of the wickedness of my People Israel. And now, because you have done all these works," says the L*ORD, "and I spoke to you, rising up early and speaking, but you did not hear, and I called you, but you did not answer, therefore I will do to the house which is called by My name, in which you trust, and to this place which I gave to you and your fathers, as I have done to Shiloh."*

—JEREMIAH 7:11-14

You shall not steal.

—EXODUS 20:15

ON THE SURFACE it seems that this commandment would be fairly easy to obey. Just don't take what doesn't belong to you, and you're doing fine. But if you take a closer look, you will discover that there are many types of stealing, some of which are engaged in by people who consider themselves to be good Christians. Stealing, you see, isn't always easy to recognize:

Consider the woman who thinks nothing of bringing supplies from her office to use at home—pens, pencils, paper, staples, paper clips. She doesn't consider it stealing, but what else would you call it?

Meanwhile, there is the man who runs cable from downstairs to the television set upstairs in his bedroom. He thinks he's clever because he has avoided paying an extra ten dollars a month to the cable company. He never stops to think that he might as well be stealing that ten dollars right out of the cable company's cash register.

Then there's the woman who calls in to work to say she isn't coming in because she is sick. The truth is, she wants to spend the day shopping with a friend and so she steals eight hours of sick pay from her employer.

Then there are the men and women who take payments "under the table" so they can underreport their income on tax returns.

You see, stealing does not merely involve picking up something that doesn't belong to you, sticking it in your pocket, and walking off with it.

Stealing comes in many shapes and varieties, and unless you are paying careful attention, some of the shapes and varieties are difficult to see.

A recent survey of a number of large organizations revealed that the average employee steals six weeks per year from his employer. How does he do this? By goofing off, coming in late, leaving early, taking extended lunches, spending extra time on coffee breaks, and hanging around the water cooler. All of this amounts to $150 billion lost to the American economy each year.

STEALING: THE GREAT AMERICAN PASTIME

Here are more interesting and disheartening figures on the amount of stealing that goes on in American society today:

- Various studies have found that three out of ten prospective employees admit to having stolen money from the previous employer. You notice that doesn't say that three out of ten stole from their employers; it says that three out of ten not only stole, but also had the audacity to admit it to the next potential employer.

- Twenty-four percent of Americans say that they have lied and cheated on their income tax, at an annual cost of about $100 billion to the government.
- Twenty-two percent of workers feel that stealing from their companies is sometimes justified.
- Thirty-three percent confess to falsely phoning in sick and collecting their sick pay.
- One-third of college students say that they would cheat on an exam if they were sure that they could get by with it, thus stealing good grades that do not belong to them.
- One in seven graduates defaults on a federal college loan, which amounts to stealing money from the government.

Just in case you think I'm pointing my finger only at workers and students, let me assure you that there are just as many studies showing how employers steal from their employees and from the public in general. Some companies steal their workers' free time from them, cutting back and cutting back and cutting back again, always trying to increase their profits at the expense of employees who are already overworked and stressed to the breaking point. This kind of work climate, in which everyone is trying unfairly to get the most out of everyone else, illustrates the problem we all face: Stealing is pandemic.

One recent survey of 500 products chosen at random revealed that approximately 50 percent of them used lies in their labeling. Packages that claimed to have 8 lobster tails contained 6. A bottle of 100 over-the-counter headache pills contained 60, and on it went through 250 packages that did not contain what the labels claimed they did.

Be careful, because you never know who is trying to steal your money.

THINGS HAVE CHANGED—FOR THE WORSE

An ancient Greek legend says that the philosopher Diogenes spent his life walking around with a lantern, looking in vain for an honest man. He might as well have been asking, "Is there one person who doesn't steal?" If Diogenes were living in America today, I have no doubt that his quest would be even more difficult than it was thousands of years ago.

Way back in the 1940s, a chain of restaurants called Toddle House implemented an honor system for paying your bill. You picked up the ticket from the counter, wrote down what you wanted, including the prices from the menu, and then added it up. When you finished eating, you dropped your ticket in a little box along with the appropriate amount of money.

A few years ago, after being closed for some time, the Toddle House restaurants reopened, using the same honor system. But it quickly became apparent that what worked so well in the 1940s and 1950s would not work today. Almost no one was paying what he really owed—and the restaurant chain was losing money fast.

As another example, consider what happened in the state of

Delaware. A new turnpike was opened, and a stack of envelopes was left under a sign at the tollbooth that said, "For those who don't have the exact change." The idea was that anyone who didn't have the right change could pick up an envelope, take it home, and then mail it in with the appropriate amount of money enclosed. That little experiment in personal honesty lasted twenty days. During that time, 26,000 people picked up an envelope instead of putting in money. Of those 26,000 envelopes, only 582 were returned, and the majority of them had blank paper or paper clips or some other kind of junk in them instead of money.

Surely, stealing has reached epidemic proportions in the last half century.

IT ALL STARTS AT HOME

There may be many reasons why stealing has gotten out of control, but I believe that most of the blame must be laid at the doorstep of the American family. Parents are not teaching their children to be honest.

I think of the little girl who was crying after being punished for taking a toy that belonged to a friend. Finally, her parents said to her, "You go in the bathroom and wash your face and stop crying." She went into the bathroom, washed her face, and dried it on the towel her parents had stolen from a Holiday Inn.

What kind of lesson did that little girl learn? Perhaps only that if you want to steal, you have to wait until you're grown up before you can get away with it.

I heard a story about a high school student who found a wallet containing a large sum of money. He was an honest young man—the kind Diogenes would have been happy to find—so he immediately took the billfold to the principal's office and turned it in. When news got out about what the young man had done, there was a great deal of discussion about it. But interestingly—or perhaps I should say sadly—no principal, no teacher, nobody connected with the school praised the young man for what he had done. They spoke about what he did as if it were quite unusual, which, in this day and age, it is. But nobody ever said it was "good."

When asked about it, one teacher said, "If I commended him for doing that, then I could no longer be his teacher. I have to be objective."

Objective? When did doing the right thing become a matter of conjecture? Does that teacher really think that there is no inherent difference between "good" and "bad" behavior—that it all depends on the observer's point of view? Would he have been just as proud of the student if he had decided to keep that money? I certainly hope not. But as this story indicates, many people in our society don't believe in moral absolutes, and a great many of them are apparently connected to our system of public education.

But I've got news for them. God's Word says there is an obvious difference between what is right and what is wrong. He says that stealing is wrong, no matter how objective we may try to be about it. If you are a parent, you can be sure that America's public schools won't help you teach your kids the difference between right and wrong—so you'd better teach them.

Personally, I find it aggravating that it costs American taxpayers billions of dollars every year to support an educational system that doesn't even know that it's wrong for students to keep things that don't belong to them. Not only is it true that Johnny can't read if he's enrolled in public school, but he probably can't tell the difference between right and wrong.

Even the people we elect to high office don't seem to know the difference between right and wrong. I saw a political cartoon that addressed this situation. The left-hand panel featured a caricature of George Washington saying, "I cannot tell a lie." In the center was Richard Nixon saying, "I cannot tell the truth." And the right-hand panel contained a caricature of Bill Clinton saying, "I cannot tell the difference."

No matter what your political point of view might be, I think you'd have to agree that the cartoonist had one valid point. Today's society is turning out people who simply cannot tell the difference between right and wrong. As far as they are concerned, the only bad thing about stealing is getting caught.

Too much of society teaches us to have distorted beliefs about stealing. We learn to justify it because "everyone does it." Some people think, *My parents did it; my employer does it; just about everyone I know does it.* Anyone who thinks that way is passing on the legacy of dishonesty and disobedience to God's Word. Is this what we want for our children? You can count on the fact that the biggest lesson they will ever learn will come from watching you.

YOU CAN'T PUT A PRICE TAG ON CHARACTER

I think of the teenaged boy whose father was trying to sell their car, which was parked out in front of the house with a For Sale sign on it. One day a stranger came to the door and made a generous offer.

The boy was excited because his dad had promised him that when they sold the car, he'd be able to buy a few things he'd wanted for a long time.

The teenager was astounded to hear his father say: "That's a very generous offer. But I ought to tell you that there are a few things you'll have to fix." Then he went on to list several items that needed repair—some of which were rather expensive.

"Wow," the stranger said. "Thanks for telling me." He stood there for a moment with his hands in his pockets, as if he didn't quite know what to do. Then he said, "I'm sorry, but in light of what you just told me, I don't think it's the car I'm looking for."

As you can imagine, the boy was very disappointed, and you may imagine the young man thought his father was foolish for blowing that deal.

You would be wrong. As the years went by, on several occasions that father heard his son say proudly, "My father is an honest man." That boy took pride in his father's honesty, and he did his best to demonstrate the same type of honesty in his own life. He learned something from his father that he never forgot: Anyone can be honest when there is nothing at stake, but it takes real integrity to be honest when it's going to cost you something.

Can you say about your father what the boy in our story said about his dad?

Here is an even more important question: Can your children say that about you? Some things in life are worth much more than dollars and cents.

The young man lost momentarily and in monetary terms—that is, in his ability to buy whatever temporal stuff he would have used the money for. But in the long run, the things he bought would have run down, decayed, broken, and eventually been tossed into the garbage can. What he got from his honest father was character—and that is lasting.

WHY DO PEOPLE STEAL?

Certainly, character is something our world could use a whole lot more of. Why is it so obviously lacking in these earliest days of the twenty-first century? In short, why do people steal? I believe there are several reasons.

First, people steal because they don't know God's Word.

You cannot do away with the Ten Commandments, you cannot do away with the Bible, you cannot do away with prayer in our schools and in the public arena—as our society has tried to do—without having a very serious erosion of morality.

The Word of God commands us not to steal. Therefore, if you know God's Word, you will know that it is wrong to take what does not belong to you.

We all need to remain in the Word of God to keep from being swallowed up by the wisdom of the world, which justifies things such as dishonesty and stealing.

Second, people steal because they think they can keep the Ten Commandments without God's help.

I cannot even begin to count the number of people who have told me over the years that they believe they have no need for

Christ's sacrifice—that they will be accepted into Heaven because they have kept the Ten Commandments. I venture to say that at least 80 percent of those people couldn't even name the Ten Commandments, much less keep them. Most of them would be hard-pressed to repeat half of the Ten Commandments, yet they have the blatant audacity to claim to have kept them.

The truth is that not one of us has kept the commandments. In thought and word and deed we have broken all of them. In omission and commission we have broken all of them. My authority for that statement is Someone who has watched your every deed, who has listened to your every word, who has heard your every thought. That is the Creator of the universe, Jesus Christ, who said, "Did not Moses give you the law, yet none of you keeps the law?" (John 7:19).

We are guilty of breaking the Ten Commandments. Therefore, we stand in need of the mercy and grace and forgiveness of God. We must depend upon God daily for help in keeping His commandments. I urge you to pray that He will help you avoid situations where you are tempted to take what does not belong to you. (After all, the Lord's Prayer asks that we should not be led into temptation.) Ask Him to help you to deal fairly with your employer or your employees, or the other people with whom you interact on a daily basis. Only with God's help can any of us become the honest, faithful people we desire to be.

Third, some people think it's okay to steal if they don't get caught.

The old saying tells us, "Crime doesn't pay." The truth is that crime sometimes does pay—temporarily. And that's the key. Any benefit derived from stealing will last only a short time. The punishment God hands out to unrepentant thieves will last an eternity.

God sees everything we do, so no one can possibly get away with stealing. People who think they can fool God mistake mercy for ignorance. He knows what they have done. He just wants to give them time to repent.

Robert Ingersoll was the most outspoken atheist of the latter half of the nineteenth century. He engaged in many public debates on God's existence, and in one such appearance, he challenged God to strike him dead within the next two minutes. The time ticked by. Two women in the audience fainted. But nothing happened to Robert Ingersoll. "You see!" he shouted. "God does not exist!"

Like many today, Robert Ingersoll did not understand the extent of God's mercy. In 2 Peter 3:9, the apostle tells us that God is patient because He does not want anyone to perish. But some people insist on choosing death over life. People who think they have gotten away with stealing are sadly mistaken. God's patience is great, but it has its limits, and then it will be "a fearful thing to fall into the hands of the living God" (Hebrews 10:31).

Admittedly, some people get caught more quickly than others do.

I heard about one man who walked into a bank, went up to a check-cashing window, and pretended to be writing out a check. Then he handed the teller a note, which read, "Give me all of your money." She did as he asked, and he left the bank with a big bag full of cash. At that point the teller turned the note over and saw that the man had written it on the back of his personal check, which had his name and address printed on it. The police were already waiting for him by the time he got home.

Then there was the young man who was hauled into court for having stolen somebody's watch, and he argued very persuasively that it was a case of mistaken identity. The judge believed him and said, "Case dismissed. You are exonerated." The defendant just stood there, shuffling back and forth from one foot to the other, so the judge repeated himself: "I said you are exonerated."

Unfortunately for the young man, his vocabulary did not include the word "exonerated." He shuffled a few seconds more and then spoke: "So . . . umm . . . does that mean I have to give back the watch?"

Foolish? Yes, but even the most clever thieves will appear just as foolish when they stand before God.

Fourth, some steal merely because they can.

In other words, "It's not my fault that he left his possessions right out in the open where I could get to them." These people seem to think that if they can steal something, they should steal it.

Over the last few years, I've met some businesspeople who think this way. Their attitude is, "If the guy doesn't know the market and doesn't know he can get the product/service better and cheaper elsewhere, then it's okay for me to 'pick his pocket.'" It's a kind of thinking that goes: "If the client doesn't know he's getting ripped off, it won't hurt him. If he finds out, it will just make him wise up. It's his problem if he is unwise in the ways of the world, and in the ways of this business in particular." After all, as the old saying goes, "Buyer beware."

There are many other reasons why people steal:

- "Because I've worked hard and I haven't been fairly rewarded for my efforts."
- "Because I need it more than they do."
- "Because I can't help myself."
- "Because I'm jealous of their success."
- "Because they don't appreciate it, and I will."
- "Because it's easier to steal something than to work for it."

I could go on for pages, but I could never come up with a valid excuse, one that circumvents the straightforward commandment of God: "You shall not steal."

In Ephesians 4:28, Paul expounds on this: "Let him who stole steal no longer, but rather let him labor, working with his hands what is good, that he may have something to give him who has need." So we are to be honest, we are to be generous, and we are to help others in need.

Most stealing is an act of commission. Yet when we are able to help our needy brothers and sisters in Christ, but refuse to do so, we are guilty of stealing through omission. In other words, if your elderly parents are in need, but you refuse to help them—even though you could—because you think they should have done a better job of preparing for their retirement years, you are stealing from them. If there is a poor single mother in your church who can't afford to buy decent clothes for her kids, and you turn away from her because you plan to use your overflowing bank account for a trip to Disney World, you are guilty. Anytime God calls you to help someone, and you refuse to do it, you are guilty.

ARE YOU STEALING FROM GOD?

A discussion of this eighth commandment would not be complete unless we talked about stealing from God.

This has to be the most heinous of all thefts because it involves stealing from the One who gave us life, the One who enables us to take each breath of our lives, the One who has provided us all things that are needful for our existence.

Speaking through the prophet Malachi, God told the Israelites: "You are cursed with a curse, for you have robbed Me, even this whole nation" (3:9).

When the people asked how they had robbed Him, He replied that they had not brought the tithes and offerings that rightfully belonged to Him.

Today we can steal from God in the same way and in many other ways as well:

- We steal from God when we refuse to set aside even one hour a week to worship Him.
- We steal from Him when we do not spend time with Him on a daily basis.
- We steal from Him when we fail to strive to develop the potential He has placed within us.

- We steal from Him when we call ourselves Christians and then fail to live up to the calling that name implies.

These are just some of the many ways we can be guilty of stealing from the Almighty.

Please examine yourself today and see if you are guilty of stealing from God or from anyone else. If you are guilty, remember that Jesus Christ can set you free.

Remember that the firstfruits of His redemption were given to a thief, the one who was crucified alongside Christ and who said, "Lord, remember me when You come into Your kingdom." Without hesitation, Jesus replied, "Assuredly, I say to you, today you will be with Me in Paradise" (Luke 23:42-43).

Christ is the Friend and Redeemer of sinners of every sort. Turn to Him, and He will wash you whiter than snow.

No matter what you may have done, His blood will cleanse you, set you free, and allow you to stand righteous and perfect before your heavenly Father.

O Blessed Lord of thieves and Friend of sinners—we pray even now that You will wash us afresh in Your precious blood. Clothe us anew in the white robes of Your perfect righteousness that we may receive the free gift of forgiveness and eternal life, that we may stand faultless before Your throne. In Your name we ask. Amen.

CHAPTER TEN

To Tell the Truth

A certain man named Ananias, with Sapphira his wife, sold a possession. And he kept back part of the proceeds, his wife also being aware of it, and brought a certain part and laid it at the apostles' feet.

But Peter said, "Ananias, why has Satan filled your heart to lie to the Holy Spirit and keep back part of the price of the land for yourself? While it remained, was it not your own? And after it was sold, was it not in your own control? Why have you conceived this thing in your heart? You have not lied to men but to God."

Then Ananias, hearing these words, fell down and breathed his last. So great fear came upon all those who heard these things.

—ACTS 5:1-5

You shall not bear false witness against your neighbor.

—Exodus 20:16

NOT VERY LONG ago, it so happened that just about every time you turned on the television, you immediately saw the serious face of now former President Clinton. If you remember that moment in presidential history, you will recall how he stared straight into the camera and, with a sincere look, denied charges that he had been involved in a sexual relationship with Monica Lewinsky. He denied it again and again and again.

But in time the truth came out. It almost always does, and when it does, if the truth reveals a lie, it is very damaging. It damages not only the reputation of the one who lied; it usually damages others as well. In President Clinton's case, the one who was lying was, at that time, the most powerful man in the world. His lies, when exposed, brought shame and discredit upon himself, his family, his office, and his country.

Telling lies is a serious offense to God. Otherwise He would not have included a commandment that strictly prohibits the telling of lies. The "lying tongue," we learn in Scripture, is an "abomination" unto the Lord (Proverbs 6:16-17). If there is one theme we have seen throughout our study of the Ten Commandments, it is this: Mankind does not take seriously the sins that most offend God. Certainly, this seems true when it comes to this, the ninth commandment, because lying is so commonplace today that people are sometimes ridiculed for being truthful.

YOUR SIN WILL FIND YOU OUT

If lying is so acceptable these days, does that mean we can lie anytime we feel like it—and get away with it? Not at all. The Bible warns us: "Be sure your sin will find you out" (Numbers 32:23).

Recently, I heard the story of a woman who married a man who claimed to be a Christian. He convinced this woman that he was a successful businessman—a millionaire, in fact. She was ecstatically happy and looked forward to a secure, wonderful life with this man. But after the vows were said and she was living with him, disturbing clues began to surface. As it turned out, her husband was not a Christian. He was a lying philanderer who took her for all she was worth. His "successful business" turned out to be far less lucrative than he had claimed. He essentially had no money. The woman was devastated! Not just because she found herself in financial ruin, but because the man she had fallen in love with, and who claimed to love her, was a liar. How could she trust him—or anyone else—ever again?

Lies not only destroy people's trust in us. They also label us as untrustworthy. Once a person's lies are exposed, the stigma of being a "liar" goes with him. People do not trust a liar. How can they? There is always a question about a person's truthfulness, once he has been caught in a lie, and the stigma generally lasts a lifetime.

In case you think I am just opinionated, let me cite the words of someone who has been well-respected throughout centuries of human history. His name was Aristotle. When asked to assess the gains or losses of lying, Aristotle said, "Hereafter the liar will not be credited, even when he speaks the truth." No one takes a liar seriously.

TO LIE, OR NOT TO LIE

People can think of all kinds of reasons to justify the lies in their lives. Many people build their lives and businesses entirely around lies. If confronted, they will explain that lying is a necessary evil in our society. People are convinced that lying is expedient—even mandatory—to be able to fit in and make a living in this world. The following poem illustrates this theme:

> A man must live! We justify
> Low shift and trick to treason high,
> A little vote for a little gold,
> Or a whole Senate bought and sold,
> With this self-evident reply.
> But is it so? Pray tell me why
> Life at such a cost you have to buy.
> In what religion were you told
> "A man must live"?

There are times when a man must die!
Imagine for a battle cry
From soldiers with a sword to hold,
From soldiers with a flag unrolled,
This coward's whine, this liar's lie,
"A man must live!"

—Charlotte Gilman

But must we really lie to make it in this world? What about God? Have we forgotten that He is in the equation and commands us not to lie?

The prophet Isaiah asked, "Of whom have you been afraid, or feared, that you have lied?" (Isaiah 57:11). Many lies are told because of fear of being put down or ridiculed. This is simply a lack of faith that God will be with us and help us if we tell the truth, and yet He will. He does help us if we tell the truth.

GOD IS TRUTH

A lie is a very serious matter to God for the very simple reason that He is truthful. Truth is inherent in God's nature, and we should be very thankful for this. If God were not true—if His Word were not absolute and firm forever—then neither would the laws of His universe be reliable and subject to scientific investigation. We would have only chaos. That's an important principle to remember: A lie brings chaos into the real world. It confuses people and causes them to base decisions on unreality. In the end it will all collapse. Likewise, if God had not impressed upon the physical world natural laws that are fixed, uniform, and universal in their application—laws that, so to speak, do not "lie"—science would be impossible. Attempts to investigate nature would yield only confusion from contradictory results. Ours would be a random universe, in fact no universe at all.

It was only because of our belief in a true and rational God whose laws could be trusted that the scientific age emerged in the Middle Ages. If His natural laws are not based on truth, anything goes. What goes down today may go up tomorrow. What boils at one temperature today may boil at another tomorrow. You see, God's truth is the very foundation upon which our world and our universe are built.

WHY WE LIE

Why do people lie? There are two reasons we will think about here.

One reason is that people are cynical by nature. These people balk at the truth. There may be any number of reasons for this. Perhaps they've been the victims of lies by key people in their lives so that they've become suspicious of anyone who even claims to tell the truth. Perhaps they are afraid to trust anyone again because of events in their lives or actions committed against them by other people.

Pontius Pilate was a cynic. During Jesus' trial, this man stood right in front of Christ and asked: "What is truth?" (John 18:38). I can just hear the challenge and sarcasm in Pilate's voice as he posed this question to Christ, who is Truth Incarnate! There was no point in Jesus' answering Pilate, because the way he posed the question revealed that the locks were sealed around his heart. He was too suspicious of the truth to recognize it if he heard it. Pilate's cynicism is echoed today in the premise of postmodernists, philosophers, and scholars who say there is no truth. In saying that, they reveal only that they don't want to know the Truth Incarnate—the Lord Jesus Christ.

Peggy Noonan, a speechwriter for the late President Ronald Reagan, once said, "Cynicism is not realistic and tough. It's unrealistic and kind of cowardly, because it means you don't have to try."

Try what? You don't have to try to navigate through life in the real world. You don't have to make any effort to believe the truth. And if you don't believe the truth, you also don't know it—therefore, you cannot be truthful. Why even try? You have a mask to hide behind. Your cynicism allows you to use lies as a shield so you can do what you want to get what you want—at someone else's expense.

A familiar example is the husband who lies to his wife, pretending he is happily married. He uses this lie as a cover-up, while he sneaks around having an affair. Basically, this man is a coward. When he is caught, he may toss his cynicism in everyone's face, saying something like, "Life is hard. I made a wrong choice when I was young. I married the wrong person. She doesn't meet my needs anymore. But who cares anyway? The world is shot, and Christian morality is outdated. I bet you would do the same thing if you were in my place."

What are the consequences of cynicism? Let us use this example to look at some of them. This man is bitter, cynical, passing the buck, rather than admitting his culpability. He is in denial, not dealing with the truth. He may think he has made a brave choice, but in reality he has been only a liar and a coward. Unless he faces his lies, he will never know the liberation of living a truthful life. He will stew in his guilt—whether he admits it or not—for the rest of his life.

A second reason we lie is that Satan lies to us, and his lies lure us far from the truth. If only we would stay focused on God's Word, which is Truth, we would not be so prone to listening to Satan. But when he craftily insinuates that perhaps God has not told us everything we need to know—or that we have misunderstood what He said—we become easily swayed. Remember the very first time Satan tricked a person with a lie? It was in response to Eve's recitation of God's truthful instructions to her. She told Satan firmly, "God has said, 'You shall not eat it, nor shall you touch it, lest you die' " (Genesis 3:3). She knew the truth.

But Satan sneered at her and told her a lie that she chose to believe. He said, "Ye shall not surely die" (Genesis 3:4 NKJV). That was the first human sin ever committed. It was a lie that continues to resonate with humankind today. The idea that we can be gods in and of ourselves and can live forever continues to hinder us in our Christian walk today.

Is it not interesting that God is Truth, Jesus Christ is Truth, and God's Word is Truth—but we don't take any of that seriously? We follow Satan—not God. Jesus bluntly confronted the hypocritical Pharisees about this issue. He said to them, "You do the works of your father, who is the devil" (John 8:44, paraphrased). Wouldn't you be angry if someone said that to you?

But the bottom line is that you are part of the family of Christ and God, or you are a child of Satan.

HOMEWARD BOUND

The family you belong to will determine your eternal destiny, so today I ask you a very important question: Are you a child of God or a child of Satan? Furthermore, I ask you this: Are you a liar? Think carefully about this, because lying has an eternal impact on you. It may even determine your eternal destiny.

First of all, we lie because we do not trust God to help us live in the truth. In essence, our lies separate us from God and prevent us from enjoying His presence and power in our daily lives. And we can do this—day after day, year after year—until we come to the end of our lives. Perhaps you have read the description of Heaven in the last two chapters of the Bible. They describe the glory of Heaven—and the Holy City, the New Jerusalem—prepared for God's children as a bride for her husband. If by grace we have chosen to be reconciled with God through Jesus Christ, we can be sure that death will be our transport into this glorious place.

However, two chapters in the Bible, as well as scores of other scriptural passages, issue a grave warning about the consequences of lying. Revelation 21:8 states, "The cowardly, unbelieving, abominable, murderers, sexually immoral, sorcerers, idolaters, and all liars shall have their part in the lake which burns with fire and brimstone, which is the second death." The text continues, "But there shall by no means enter it anything that defiles, or causes an abomination or a lie, but only those who are written in the Lamb's Book of Life" (v. 27). Just a few verses from the end of the Bible, we read a description of those who will ultimately be destined to remain forever outside the Holy City: "Outside are dogs and sorcerers and sexually immoral and murderers and idolaters, and whoever loves and practices a lie" (Revelation 22:15).

Wouldn't you agree that God gives us fair warning about where our lies will lead us? Are lies in your life causing you to dwell in the kingdom of the devil?

Please be advised that if you lie and do not sincerely repent and receive cleansing by the blood of Jesus Christ, your lies can keep you out of heaven.

WAYS WE LIE

As you are reading this chapter, perhaps you are thinking about the way the ninth commandment is phrased: "You shall not bear false witness against your neighbor." To feel that this instruction applies to you, you must understand what "bearing false witness" means. It does not refer just to standing up in a courtroom and testifying falsely about someone who has been accused of a crime. Bearing false witness includes telling untruths about or to other people anywhere in life.

We have been talking about our natural kinship with Satan, the devil. The Greek word for "devil" is *diabolos*. It comes from the words *bolos,* which means "to throw," and *dia,* which means "through." So we see that "devil" means "to pierce through," as with a dart. Satan is an expert at hurling accusations—like darts—at people. I'm sorry to say it, but so are we.

How do we hurl the darts of lies?

Accusations are one effective way we bring false witness against other people. Sometimes, of course, accusations are true. But we break the ninth commandment when we damage another person through false accusations, especially when we speak falsely to a third party. Let me give you an example:

Let us say that a man named Joe is angry at his friend Jennifer. She told him she was going to play golf with him on Saturday but never bothered to call him. At work on Monday, Joe takes a coffee break with Jim and tells him not to trust Jennifer. She's always saying she'll do something, but not carrying through. After this, Jim avoids Jennifer because he thinks she's "bad news." Her feelings are really hurt when he acts cool and unfriendly. She has no idea why.

This is a very simple illustration of how we can poison other people's minds toward someone by casually talking about her. The worst part is that Joe never went directly to Jennifer to ask her why she didn't call. There might have been a good reason, but he didn't give her a chance to explain.

Of course, there are many other ways to accuse people. We can do it through outright gossip or subtle insinuations. We can do it through angry, irrational outbursts to a person's face. We even accuse people falsely by merely believing something we've heard—without giving the accused the courtesy of being allowed to defend themselves.

It is reported that Saint Augustine had a sign on his desk that said, "Whosoever enters this office to bring accusation against his brother will be ushered out of this room." Obviously, Saint Augustine took the ninth commandment seriously! And so should we. To maliciously accuse someone is terribly hurtful, and that is the emphasis of the ninth commandment. God is offended when we lash out at a "neighbor." Many scriptural passages deal with lying in other forms, but here God is pinpointing a type of lie that hurts other people. This is the most malicious.

Slander is another way we bear false witness. When we slander someone, we intentionally set out to tell falsehoods about that person. It is an entirely indirect attack. Through slander, we can destroy another person without even seeing him, without speaking to him, without touching him, by destroying his reputation in the community, in the office, or in the church. It is easy enough to do. Just by elaborating on something you don't like about a person or by embellishing a flaw in that person's character, you can turn people against him in a flash.

Scripture records and condemns many instances of slander. Joseph, Jeremiah, and John the Baptist suffered deeply because others slandered their good names. And Jesus Christ Himself, the only perfect man who ever lived, had the vile cloak of slander thrown around His shoulder. Listen to some of the vile words used to slander our Savior:

> Look, a glutton and a winebibber, a friend of tax collectors and sinners! (Luke 7:34).
>
> "He has Beelzebub," and, "By the ruler of the demons He casts out demons" (Mark 3:22).
>
> This Man blasphemes! (Matthew 9:3).

Slander is often the product of envy. When we are jealous of others' popularity, success, or capabilities, we sometimes slander them in an attempt to make ourselves look good. Lord Byron once said, "If you aspire to climb to the height of the mountain, you will look down upon the hatred of those beneath you."

Denigration is still another way we bear false witness. Denigration means to emphasize negative attributes about a person so much that we leave an impression that there is just nothing good about that person.

Whenever Peter the Great heard someone denigrating another person, he responded, "Ah, yes, but is there nothing good about him?" In a subtle way, he was saying that we should look for the good rather than the bad in people.

There is a flip side to this. Do people come to you and tell you all kinds of terrible things about others? If so, perhaps you need to examine yourself and see whether you encourage others to bear false witness in this way. I've never forgotten a comment Bill Bright made more than thirty years ago. He said, "People don't dump garbage on green lawns." How true! They dump garbage on vacant lots filled with rocks and sand and weeds. Do you invite garbage dumping?

The Bible warns against having an eager ear to hear slander. In fact, Proverbs tells us "*do not associate with a gossip*" (Proverbs 20:19 NASB). Do you lend an eager ear when someone hurls an accusation? Do you perk up with interest when you hear a word of slander or denigration? If you will take a stand one time by saying that you really don't want to hear these comments, you probably won't be invited to listen to them anymore! And I want you to know this: You will be blessed.

TAKING IT PERSONALLY

Perhaps as you have been reading this chapter, the Holy Spirit has been convicting you. You have a problem with this commandment. You have accused someone falsely . . . slandered someone's good name . . . gossiped about a friend. As with every other sin, there is hope for release from this one. Because of the atoning sacrifice of Jesus Christ, God can forgive you. And if you are truly repentant, He can change you and eradicate this sin from your life.

Back in the 1970s, a young woman committed a terrible crime. She murdered a policeman, then vanished to the West Coast. She was never caught, and the case remained unsolved. She lived her life as a model citizen, and no one who knew her suspected she was a murderer. She could have gotten away with this crime, except for one thing: Guilt. Her guilty conscience would not leave her alone. She was tormented day and night by her secret sin because, you see, it was no secret to God. Finally, the woman confessed and turned herself in. It was only in acknowledging the wrong she committed that she could be free of the guilt. When she made the decision to come clean, she was released from the torture within. Whatever consequence she had to face, it would be better than living a lie.

I'm sure you harbor no secret as dreadful as this, but if you are tormented because you have broken God's ninth commandment and your heart is grieved, come clean with God right now. Pray the prayer here, filling in your personal details and acknowledging the cleansing blood of Jesus Christ. He will welcome you home—to the dwelling place of Truth.

Heavenly Father, my conscience has been pricked; my heart has been pierced by Your Spirit. I stand before You now, convicted of my sin. It has been said that there is nothing wrong with our tongues that a change of heart wouldn't cure.

I pray, O God, that You will change my heart. Make mine a heart full of love and blessings. Cleanse my mouth of all curses and slander. Make me, O Christ, more like You, who are Truth Incarnate. In Your name. Amen.

CHAPTER ELEVEN

The Gate of the Heart

It came to pass after these things that Naboth the Jezreelite had a vineyard which was in Jezreel, next to the palace of Ahab king of Samaria. So Ahab spoke to Naboth, saying, "Give me your vineyard, that I may have it for a vegetable garden, because it is near, next to my house; and for it I will give you a vineyard better than it. Or, if it seems good to you, I will give you its worth in money."

But Naboth said to Ahab, "The LORD forbid that I should give the inheritance of my fathers to you!"

So Ahab went into his house sullen and displeased because of the word which Naboth the Jezreelite had spoken to him; for he had said, "I will not give you the inheritance of my fathers." And he lay down on his bed, and turned away his face, and would eat no food.

—1 KINGS 21:1-4

You shall not covet your neighbor's house; you shall not covet your neighbor's wife, nor his male servant, nor his female servant, nor his ox, nor his donkey, nor anything that is your neighbor's.

—EXODUS 20:17

THE TENTH COMMANDMENT has been called the commandment that nobody breaks, or the sin that no one commits. One Roman Catholic priest said he had been listening to confessions for fifty years, but had never heard anybody confess to having broken the tenth commandment. And a Protestant pastor, from a congregation where sins are confessed openly at prayer meeting, stated that he had never heard anyone confess to the sin of covetousness.

Does this mean people don't commit this sin anymore?

Hardly!

Have you seen the bumper sticker, "He who dies with the most toys wins"?

The truth is that American society today is filled with people who are constantly striving to accumulate more toys—bigger, better, fancier cars, boats, home entertainment systems, and just about everything else you can name—simply because they covet whatever anyone else has.

Advertisers play to our covetous nature:

"You can have it all!"

"Sure it costs more, but you're worth it!"

They do it because it works!

In the twelfth chapter of Luke, Christ said, "Beware of covetousness" (v. 15), and yet most people today don't give it a second thought. We are like fish that don't think about the water in which they swim. We are so immersed in covetousness that we don't even notice it.

Christ told us we are not to seek anxiously after the things of this world: "Do not worry, saying, 'What shall we eat?' or 'What shall we drink?' or 'What shall we wear?' For after all these things the Gentiles seek. For your heavenly Father knows that you need all these things. But seek first the kingdom of God and His righteousness, and all these things shall be added to you" (Matthew 6:31-33).

Covetousness is not the same thing as ambition, the God-given desire to be the best person you can possibly be. Covetousness is the inordinate desire for the things of this world. Who is the covetous person? He who spends his whole life muckraking in the mud flats of materialism, when God created us for the stars. It is the person who never seeks anything beyond the shiny, ultimately worthless baubles of this life.

THE CONSEQUENCES OF COVETOUSNESS

Some people shrug off covetousness as if it's a minor offense, relatively harmless. That is not so. Left unchecked, covetousness can lead to terrible evil. It can even lead to murder. (I urge you to turn to the book of 1 Kings 21 and read the story.)

Not too long ago, a fifteen-year-old boy left home on a bright, clear morning wearing a brand-new pair of gym shoes, and they were a wonder to behold. They had everything but bells and whistles, and they cost his mother a hundred dollars. They also cost the boy his life. The next day a seventeen-year-old left his home wearing those same shoes. Shortly after that, the body of the fifteen-year-old was found among the weeds of a vacant lot, and his shoes were missing. In that same school district, three other children were killed for their clothing that year.

Children will do almost anything to have brand-name clothing. Some will even kill for it. This is covetousness run amok, and it is a very dangerous thing.

A MATTER OF THE HEART

And yet, if you examine the laws of Egypt, Babylonia, Greece, Rome, or any other ancient society, you will find nothing that remotely resembles the prohibition against covetousness. Why? Because most laws—including the other nine commandments—deal with things in the external world, but this one deals with the internal workings of the human heart.

Edith Schaeffer, widow of the famed theologian Francis Schaeffer, says that this commandment deals with the inside of the cup. She is referring to the fact that Jesus condemned the

Pharisees because they cleaned the outside of the platter and the cup, but left the inside filled with all kinds of vileness and wickedness (Matthew 23: 25-26).

The Pharisees kept all of the various details of the law. They tithed mint and anise and cumin. They tithed the little plants in their gardens, but their hearts were unclean, and God will never be satisfied with religiosity, with churchmanship. He is looking for a pure heart.

I think of nine-year-old Johnny, who became angry about something in his classroom at school. There he stood, arms crossed, tapping his foot on the floor. His teacher came over to him and said, "Johnny, sit down," but he wouldn't do it.

Finally, she had had enough of his behavior and shouted at him, "Johnny, sit down now!"

As he slowly sank into his chair, he grumbled, "I may be sitting down on the outside, but inside I'm standing up."

His body was obeying, but his heart wasn't.

You see, God knows when we're standing up on the inside. He looks upon the heart. He hears our thoughts, and that is why He says things like this:

> Set your mind on things above, not on things on the earth. . . . Therefore put to death your members which are on the earth: fornication, uncleanness, passion, evil desire, and covetousness, which is idolatry. Because of these things the wrath of God is coming upon the sons of disobedience" (Colossians 3:2, 5-6).

God knows there are certain things you need, and He will provide them: food, clothing, shelter, water, people who care about you. These are just a few of the basic needs common to all people.

But some people become so covetous and so greedy for the things of this life that they make themselves miserable.

Do you know what the opposite of covetousness is? Contentment. The covetous man is never satisfied. When someone asked John D. Rockefeller, "How much money would be enough?" he replied, "Just a little bit more."

That is the nature of covetousness. It always wants something more.

How about you? Is your heart set on the things above or the things below? The reason so many church members are of little value to the kingdom of God is that all of their desires are set on things below. The Bible tells us, "Do not love the world or the things in the world. If anyone loves the world, the love of the Father is not in him" (1 John 2:15).

The problem with most Christians is not that they want too much, but that they want too much of the wrong things. A few years ago, I was looking for a birthday card for my daughter, and I came across one that said, "Where would I ever find a daughter like you?"

I thought, *What a nice sentiment. Just what I wanted to say.* But then I opened it and looked inside. "I don't know," it said, "but the mall would be a good place to start."

How sad that some people think the best of life can be found in a shopping mall!

In traffic recently, I was behind a car with a bumper sticker that proclaimed, "Born to shop." I thought, *It's so sad that anyone would think the primary purpose of life would be to pursue the accumulation of things.*

How I wish that all professing Christians desired less of the world and more of God's kingdom. I wish they were zealous for the glory of God and the advancement of His kingdom. If that were the case, I know we could reach the entire world for Jesus Christ!

LET GOD CHANGE YOUR "WANTER"

There was a time when I was attracted to the things of this world. But then, about forty years ago, Christ put a screwdriver into my "wanter" and simply turned it upside down. Suddenly, I found myself wanting things I had never wanted before—and not wanting things I had always wanted before. Does your "wanter" need to be changed? If so, ask Him to fix it so that you desire first His kingdom and His righteousness. He can do that for you if by His grace you will let Him.

It doesn't matter how scrupulous a Pharisee you may become; you are not going to make it into heaven if your heart is full of sin. Only God can see the desires of the human heart. And only Christ can change them.

Many years ago, when men were clearing the land in this country for farmland, they had a big problem trying to get rid of the stumps—especially when a stump went down into a vast system of roots. Finally, somebody invented a stump hook. This big machine had four iron hooks that came down on all four sides and hooked into the stump of the tree. Then, through a series of mechanisms and levers, it would rip that stump right out of the ground—roots and all.

That is what becoming a Christian is all about. Christ sent His Spirit to act as a "Stump Hook," to root out all the wicked desires of our hearts so that our affections would be set completely upon Him.

You see, all sin begins in the heart. Jesus said, "Out of the heart proceed evil thoughts, murders, adulteries, fornications, thefts, false witness, blasphemies" (Matthew 15:19).

It is when sin is still in the thought stage that you must rebuke Satan and ask Christ to deliver you—before that sin takes root and produces its deadly fruit.

As Martin Luther said, "We can't keep the birds from flying over our heads, but we can keep them from nesting in our hair."

A FINAL LOOK AT COVETOUSNESS

At the beginning of this chapter I mentioned that covetousness is the sin nobody talks about. That's because no one seems to recognize it, and that makes it one of the most dangerous of all sins. It can have you completely in its grip before you even see it coming!

Every day you are being bombarded by billions of dollars' worth of advertising designed to encourage you to covet. But if you give in, you will never be satisfied. You are always going to want just a little bit more.

Contentment with godliness is great gain. Paul said, "I have learned in whatever state I am, to be content: I know how to be abased, and I know how to abound" (Philippians 4:11-12).

Contentment. How glorious it is! And it comes from setting your heart on the things of God.

You cannot love both God and mammon.
Set your heart on God, and your spirit will soar!

Lord Jesus, You have said, "Beware of covetousness." You have told us to flee temptation. We pray that we might be cleansed by Your blood, that we might be made whiter than snow. Wash the inside of the cup that we may not be as the Pharisees, who deluded themselves into thinking they were righteous, when You saw their hearts as full of all manner of evil. Deliver us, we pray, from the very desire for sin. Fix our affections upon things that are above and not upon things below. Make us truly Your own, for we pray this, O Christ, in Your most holy and gracious name. Amen.

EPILOGUE: LAW AND GOSPEL

Do we then make void the law through faith? Certainly not! On the contrary, we establish the law.

—ROMANS 3:31

Imagine for a moment that you lived in the last century, when horses and buggies were commonplace. One day you step outside into the street and see a few people with their horses and buggies, riding up and down very comfortably. But then, to your amazement, you see a great crowd of people sitting in their buggies, but the horses are not hitched up in front as usual. The horses are somehow rigged up behind the buggies. Those in the buggies are saying, with great frustration and irritation, "Giddyap, boy! Push! Push!"

You would think, *How incredibly stupid can these folks be! This can never work,* and you would be right.

You would be witnessing a classic case of what's called getting the cart before the horse. Because the order is all wrong, all that can come of a situation like that is the utter frustration and futility of trying harder and harder to make something work that can never work.

THE BACKWARD GOSPEL

Sadly, the vast majority of people today—if they have heard the Gospel at all—have gotten it backward. They may even be Christians, in that they have surrendered their lives to Jesus Christ and trust in His atoning sacrifice on the Cross to cover their sins. Although they have salvation and an eternal place with God, they seemingly have no power in their lives to live as Christians now, glorifying God with righteous living.

This situation exists today for too many believers because they have reversed something about the Gospel. And so they are left with frustration, failure, shame, and guilt, wondering why the message of the Gospel won't work in their real experience.

To this point, we have concluded eleven chapters of studies in the law of God—specifically, the Ten Commandments that are the foundational laws of righteous living given to us by the Almighty. But before we end, it is vital that we step back and see these commandments in their right and proper context.

I am talking about our need to see the law of God in its right relationship to the Gospel of God.

THE BIBLE HAS IT RIGHT

The Bible contains basically two elements: Law and Gospel. Unless we get these in the proper relationship, one to another, we will not find ourselves in the right relationship with God. Our lives will not work, and our Christian experience will be marked by frustration and failure. Therefore, we must look carefully at the relationship of that law to the Gospel and understand how they are made to work together.

Now, in general, Christians understand that the ultimate message of the Bible is not commandments or laws. While God's laws are not just good advice (though, frankly, they are good advice, and much more!), the basic message of the whole Bible taken altogether is that God has an amazing announcement to make to each one of us. That message was proclaimed at the birth of our Lord, Jesus Christ.

On that first Christmas evening, when angels from Heaven appeared to the shepherds outside Bethlehem, one of the angels said, "I bring you good tidings of great joy which will be to all people!" (Luke 2:10). We bring you Good News!

Do we yet comprehend the wonder and glory of this Good News? The Good News is this: For those who have not even recognized God's laws for the good advice for living they contain, for those who have broken the law of the living God who made us—which is every one of us—God nonetheless offers His mercy and His grace.

The wonder and glory of the Gospel are that it is the Good News about God's amazing grace. Grace shed upon those who will acknowledge they are lawbreakers and criminals who stand guilty before the eyes of almighty God.

The absolutely amazing thing about this message of Good News is that God welcomes us, who hated and rebelled against

Him, as His own sons and daughters (see John 1), if we will bow before Him and confess our crimes of rebellion. Then is the gift of eternal life ours.

This Good News is of vast importance because without it, we human beings always put the cart before the horse in our dealings with God. We offer Him our puny sacrifices, or our tallies of good behavior, hoping our good works will be enough to turn away His anger at our rebellion and exonerate us from the penalty for rebellion we deserve.

However, the good works of man have never been enough to cover the sin and rebellion of man. Only the sacrifice of Jesus Christ—His blood shed on the Cross—has been enough to pay for our atonement.

Do you see why it is absolutely imperative that we get the order of things right? Only after you and I have received the gift of eternal life . . . only after we have trusted utterly in Christ's sacrifice for us, and nothing else . . . only after having been redeemed . . . only after we have been adopted into the family of God, do we find that the commandments of God show us how we may please our Father, who has done this great thing for us.

DO NOT SLIP BACK

However, many who belong to Christ often forget the amazing grace that has been shed upon us. They are still putting the buggy before the horse, so to speak.

Constantly, I hear frustrated, defeated Christians saying such things as, "Well, I'm trying to keep the commandments. I'm doing the best I can."

These struggling souls remind me of a woman named Mrs. Whyte, who said to her pastor: "I'm trying my best to be a Christian, but I just don't know whether I am or not."

Her pastor asked, "Are you Mrs. Whyte?"

She said, "Yes, of course, I am."

Her pastor asked, "Are you trying to be Mrs. Whyte?"

"No," she replied. "I am Mrs. Whyte. Ever since that day when I held out my hand and my husband placed the ring on my finger, I have been Mrs. Whyte."

"It is the same way," the pastor explained, "in relation to God. Ever since that day when you put your hand in the hand of the Savior, you have been a child of God. You have been a Christian. There is nothing you could do to try to become a Christian. Since that day you have been one all along. Now the laws of God fit into their right place. They are there simply to show you how to be a good Christian—that is, how to please and bring glory and honor to God by your life." There are great truths here, for those who have not entered into a relationship with God through Christ and for those who have.

THOSE WHO HAVE NOT

For those who have not entered into that marriage-type relationship with Christ . . . who have not become the bride of the heavenly Bridegroom . . . who are not part of the family . . . who are on the outside looking in—it is not enough to try to act like a good wife. "Acting like" is not the same thing as entering into a covenant relationship with a husband.

You may desire to be married to someone great and attractive and wealthy. And yet, just trying to live as if you were that person's spouse will not make you become the spouse. You must be invited into a covenant relationship and accept the ring—the token of love and fidelity—and let it be placed upon your finger.

If you have not entered into a covenant relationship with God, accepting His offering of love—which is the blood of Christ—then no amount of acting will make you His, no matter how good you may behave.

THOSE WHO HAVE

For those who have entered the covenant relationship with God, through faith . . . getting in right order the relationship of the law to the Gospel is also incredibly important. If we do not, our lives will be needlessly marred by a sense of striving, frustration, and condemnation when what we are offered, as a blessing, is peace with God.

As D. T. Niles, a founder of the East Asia Christian Conference, has observed: "In other religions, good works are done 'in order to.' In Christianity, good works are a 'therefore.'" What does this mean?

If we go back to the very first commandment, we will see. Before the first words of command were uttered to us, God said, "I am the LORD your God, who brought you out of the land of Egypt, out of the house of bondage" (Exodus 20:2).

He is, first and foremost, God, and He is our God, if we bow the knee to Him.

Then, as He commands us, there is an implicit "therefore," and we must read what comes next like this: "[Therefore] you shall have no other gods before Me" (Exodus 20:3).

In all of the world religions, man endeavors to reach up and somehow find God. In fact, the word "religion" means to "bind oneself to." Only in Christianity, however, do you find God reaching down to man. Only here does the Lord reach down to find fallen and helpless humans. Only here does God do what is necessary for us to be reconciled to Him. What does He do? He gives grace.

Grace has been poured out by God to bring us to Himself. Without grace, we cannot come to Him. And grace is poured out to help after we have come to Him as well. Without grace, we cannot continue with Him. Grace is the wondrous gift given to those who have nothing to pay; to those who do not deserve it at all. This world does not operate on grace. It operates on the basis of merit—on the basis of justice. Quid pro quo. Tit for tat. You do this; you get that.

God, the Judge of all the earth—who is not only Judge, but Sovereign Ruler as well—extends mercy and pardon. That is grace. He also extends to us help, the grace to live righteously according to His laws. That is grace also. It is the whole wondrous news of the law and the gospel together, as contained in the Bible, the Word of God.

A VISION BY WHICH YOUR SOUL MAY LIVE

Why is it imperative to get the relationship between the law and gospel in the right order? Because when we try to live by the law first, we kill the real work of grace within. We slip back into striving to please God so that He will accept us as His own. And then we make a mockery of grace. We begin to try to do what only grace can do. And so, we trample God's free offering of grace that alone can empower us to live righteous lives.

We do this, I believe, because we lose sight of the wonder of what God Himself has done for us, and what He will continue to do, if we but stay in right relation to Him by His grace.

John Bunyan, in his *Pilgrim's Progress,* offers us a literary vision that we can hold on to. Images in word form that beautifully, memorably contrast the relationship of law and gospel we need to hold onto.

In this spiritual masterpiece, the main character, Christian, is taken to a large, beautifully appointed parlor by another character called Interpreter. This room has not been dusted or swept in many and many a year, and it is thick with dust and cobwebs.

Interpreter calls in a man with a broom and asks him to sweep the room. As he sweeps, the room is filled with the dust that is stirred up, causing Christian to choke, cough, and gasp for breath. Then Interpreter calls in a maiden and bids her to sprinkle the room with water, after which the dust settles and the room is easily cleansed.

"What means this?" Christian asks Interpreter. He replies that the room "is the heart of a man that was never sanctified by the sweet grace of the Gospel. The dust is his original sin and inward corruptions that have defiled the whole man. He that began to sweep at first is the law; but she that brought water and did sprinkle it is the Gospel."

What a wonderful way Bunyan has of expressing scriptural truths! For the law was given that sin might abound (Romans 5:20). The law stirs up that sin until our spirits can hardly breathe. We choke with the sin that is blown into our faces by the law, until we are convicted and know something must be done for us.[1]

This is just the point where many a Christian, like many a non-Christian, is apt to go wrong. People who are outside Christ don't like to hear the law of God because they know they are guilty. People who are in Christ often don't like to hear the law of God because it makes them anxious and they forget that grace is there to help . . . and they return to their old way—which is always a vain and guilty striving to please God.

Bunyan again illustrates what we must do with our guilty striving. After struggling with the great, exhausting burden of guilt and sin strapped to his back, our poor Pilgrim (who is about to become Christian) makes his way to the hill of Calvary. As he climbs to the top of that hill, he sees there a Cross, and upon that Cross, One hanging who is the Son of God. As he lifts his eyes to look at that Cross, suddenly, the burden breaks loose, and this great weight of sin and guilt rolls down the hill and disappears into the dark opening of a sepulcher, never to be seen again.

Perhaps you have been to that hill of Calvary. Perhaps you have been Pilgrim, and now you are Christian. But I wonder—have you really heard the whole message of the Gospel's Good News?

Now that Christian's burden has fallen away, three bright shining beings appear to him, greeting him with, "Peace be to thee."

The first one said to him, "Thy sins be forgiven thee."

Another one strips him of the filthy, foul rags of his unrighteousness and clothes him with the white robe of Christ's perfect obedience that he might stand faultless before God.

The third gives him a sealed scroll, his guarantee of eternal Paradise with God.

What a beautiful presentation of the relationship of the law and the Gospel.

- The Law is our condemnation; the Gospel of grace is our salvation.
- The Law condemns; the Gospel justifies.
- The Law convicts; the Gospel of grace relieves.
- The Law produces rebellion in the heart; the Gospel of grace of God produces submission.
- The Law depresses us with our inability to keep it; the Gospel enlivens and delivers us from that depression and produces joy.
- The Law produces pride in those who ignorantly suppose that they have kept it; the Gospel, indeed, produces thankfulness and humility in those who know they are accepted, even though in themselves they are unacceptable. The Gospel says, "Come unto me and I will give you rest." The Gospel says, "Grace unto you and peace."
- The Law says, "Do"; the Gospel says, "Done."
- The Law says, "Go"; the Gospel says, "Come."

Grace says to you,

> Though your sins are like scarlet, they shall be as white as snow (Isaiah 1:18).

The Gospel says to you,

> I have loved you with an everlasting love (Jeremiah 31:3).
>
> [Nothing] shall be able to separate us from the love of God (Romans 8:39).
>
> Who shall bring a charge against God's elect? (Romans 8:33).

Those of us who have heard the Gospel a thousand times over must beware, lest we become Gospel hardened. We must beware of the strong pull to return to living by our own good works. We must worship and adore the one true God. Then we must continually yield and yield and yield our lives to Him . . . every day . . . every hour . . . every minute. For only as we yield, continually repenting of rebellion, living by faith, obeying Him by the power of grace . . . will we live as true sons and daughters of the living God.

As we close, I must ask: Dear friend, have you ever truly yielded your life to Christ? Have you ever truly surrendered yourself to Him? Do you need—for the first time or the ten thousandth—to yield your heart to Him?

> *Heavenly Father, for those who have been ignorant of the Gospel, but have just discovered it, and for those who have heard it a thousand times over and yet have resisted it, in either case may the Holy*

Spirit melt their hearts and draw them unto Christ. Right now, right where they are, at this moment, may all who are reading this say in their hearts:

"Lord Jesus Christ, I yield myself to You. I open my heart. Come in and cleanse and melt and woo my heart to You. Bind me with bonds of love to Your side. Help me, henceforth, from this day forward, to love You supremely, to serve You faithfully, until I come to see You face-to-face. In Your name I pray." Amen.

ENDNOTES

Introduction

1. William J. Bennett, *The Index of Leading Cultural Indicators*, Updated and Expanded Edition (New York: Broadway Books; Colorado Springs: Waterbrook Press, 1999).

2. The Barna Update, August 6, 2001; http://www.barna.org/FlexPage.aspx?Page=BarnaUpdate&BarnaUpdateID=95; accessed August 8, 2004.

3. Spirit of Revival magazine; 3/30/2001; accessed 8/18/2004 at http://www.lifeaction.org/Articles/viewarticle.asp?id=1113145058; copyright © 1996 by Nancy Leigh DeMoss.

Chapter One: Do We Need the Law of God?

1. Paul Johnson, *Modern Times: The World from the Twenties to the Nineties*, revised edition (New York: HarperCollins Publishers, 1991), pp. 1-5.

Chapter Two: The One True God

1. C. S. Lewis, *The Weight of Glory* (New York: HarperCollins, 1976), p. 26.

2. Francis Schaeffer, *The God Who Is There* (Downers Grove, Illinois: InterVarsity Press, 1968), p. 94.

3. Charles Hodge, *Systematic Theology* (Part III) (Peabody, Massachusetts: Hendrickson Publishers, 1999), p. 280.

Chapter Three: False Gods

1. Edith Schaeffer, *Hidden Art* (Carol Stream, Illinois: Tyndale House, 1972), p. 46.

2. Tatian, as quoted in *You Give Me New Life*, David Hazard, ed. (Minneapolis, Minnesota: Bethany House Publishers, 1995).

Chapter Five: The Gift of Rest
1. Ron Mehl, *The Tender Commandments* (Sisters, Oregon: Multnomah Publishers, 1998), pp.101-124.
2. Roberts and Donaldson, eds., *The Ante-Nicene Fathers* (Volume I) (Grand Rapids, Michigan: William B. Eerdmans Publishing Company), p. 147.

Chapter Seven: Thou Shalt Do No Murder
1. The five are 1) Samson in Judges 16:29-30; 2) Saul and his armor-bearer in 1 Samuel 31:4-5; 3) Ahithophel in 2 Samuel 17:23; 4) Zimri in 1 Kings 16:18; and 5) Judas in Matthew 27:5.

Chapter Eight: The Sexual Revolution
1. Randy C. Alcorn, *Restoring Sexual Sanity* (Ft. Lauderdale, Florida: Coral Ridge Ministries, 2000), p. 3.
2. Paul Lee Tan, *Encyclopedia of 7700 Illustrations: Signs of the Times* (Rockville, Maryland: Assurance Publishers, 1984), p. 793.
3. Rutgers, The State University of New Jersey, The National Marriage Project, "Should We Live Together," online at http://marriage.rutgers.edu/Publications/swlt2.pdf copyright © 2002, 1999 by the National Marriage Project.
4. Paul Cameron, Ph.D., "Medical Consequences of What Homosexuals Do," the Family Research Institute; http://familyresearchinst.org/FRI_EDUPAMPHLET3.html, accessed August 23, 2004.

Epilogue: Law and Gospel
1. John Bunyan, *The Pilgrim's Progress*; accessed online at Christian Classics Ethereal Library: http: //www.ccel.org/ccel/bunyan/pilgrim.titlepage.html.

BS 1285.52 .K46 2005
Kennedy, D. James
Why the Ten Commandments
Matter.